Classic Cocktail Guides
and Retro Bartender Books

Stuart's Fancy Drinks and How to Mix Them

Containing Clear and Practical Directions for Mixing All Kinds of Cocktails, Sours, Egg Nog, Sherry Cobblers, Coolers, Absinthe, Crustas, Fizzes, Flips, Juleps, Fixes, Punches, Lemonades, Pousse Cafes, Invalids' Drinks, Etc. Etc.

Thomas Stuart

Historic Cookbooks of the World
Kalevala Books, Chicago

"Work is the curse of the drinking class."
— Oscar Wilde, 1854–1900

Stuart's Fancy Drinks and How to Mix Them

© 2010 Compass Rose Technologies, Inc. All rights reserved. No part of this book may be reproduced in any manner whatsoever without written permission, except in the case of brief quotations embodied in critical articles and reviews. Originally published as *Stuart's Fancy Drinks and How to Mix Them* by Thomas Stuart, 1896, 1904. Title page illustration courtesy of Dover Publications, Inc., New York.

Joanne Asala, Editor
Historic Cookbooks of the World

Rowan Grier, Series Editor
Classic Cocktail Guides
and Retro Bartender Books

Classic Cocktail Guides and Retro Bartender Books and *Historic Cookbooks of the World* are published by Kalevala Books, an imprint of Compass Rose Technologies, Inc., PO Box 409095, Chicago, IL 60640. Titles published by Kalevala Books are available at special quantity discounts to use as premiums and sales promotions or for academic use. For more information, please write to the Director of Special Sales, Compass Rose Technologies, Inc., PO Box 409095, Chicago, IL 60640 or contact us through our Web site, www.CompassRose.com.

Editors' Note

Some ingredients found in vintage cocktail guides are unavailable or hard to come by today. Check out our resource guide at the back for vendors who specialize in hard-to-find ingredients and websites with information on how to recreate classic cocktails and cocktail ingredients.

ISBN: 978-1-880954-34-8

No. 77 Nov., 1904. | **Excelsior Library.** | Issued Quarterly. Subscription $1.00 Per Year.

STUART'S
FANCY DRINKS
AND
HOW TO MIX THEM.

CONTAINING

CLEAR AND PRACTICAL DIRECTIONS FOR MIXING ALL KINDS OF COCKTAILS, SOURS, EGG NOG, SHERRY COBBLERS, COOLERS, ABSINTHE, CRUSTAS, FIZZES, FLIPS, JULEPS, FIXES, PUNCHES, LEMONADES, POUSSE CAFES INVALIDS' DRINKS, ETC. ETC.

BY THOS. STUART.

NEW YORK:
EXCELSIOR PUBLISHING HOUSE,
McKeon & Schofield, Proprietors,
8 Murray Street.

Entered at Post Office, New York, N.Y., as Second-Class Matter, March 3, 1896.

COPYRIGHT, 1904,

BY

EXCELSIOR PUBLISHING HOUSE.

CONTENTS.

	PAGE.		PAGE
Absinthe	9	Brandy Fix	27
Absinthe, American style of mixing	9	Brandy Flip	30
		Brandy Fizz	28
Absinthe, French style	9	Brandy Julep	35
Absinthe, Italian style	10	Brandy Punch	46
Absinthe Cocktail	17	Brandy Sangaree	57
Ale Sangaree	57	Brandy Scaffa	13
Amaranth Cocktail	18	Brandy Sling	61
American Pousse Cafe	42	Brandy Smash	62
Apple Jack Cocktail	18	Brandy and Soda	12
Apple Jack Fix	27	Brandy Sour	64
Apple Jack Sour	64	Brandy Straight	67
Apple Toddy	87	Brandy Toddy	69
"Arf and Arf," or Black and Tan	10	Brandy Shrub	93
		Burned Brandy and Peach	12
Arrack Punch	45	Brunswick Cooler	17
Arrack Punch, "Hot"	45	California Milk Punch	76
Balaklavo Nectar	94	California Sherry Cobbler	14
Baltimore Egg Nog	25	California Wine Cobbler	15
Beef Tea	92	Canadian Punch	78
Bishop A	10	Catawba Wine Cobbler	15
Bishop a la Prusse	96	Century Club Punch	76
Black Stripe	11	Champagne Wine Cobbler	15
Blue Blazer	11	Champagne Cocktail	18
Bombay Punch	79	Champagne Cup	86
Boston Egg Nog	87	Champagne Julep	35
Bottle of Cocktail	83	Champagne Punch	46
Bottled Velvet	94	Champagne Sour	64
Bowl of Egg Nog for a party	86	Champagne Velvet	87
Brace Up	92	Cider Egg Nog	90
Brace Up, Saratoga	90	Claret Cobbler	15
Brandy Champerelle, No. 1	12	Claret Cup for a party	94
Brandy Champerelle, No. 2	13	Claret and Champagne Cup	84
Brandy and Ginger Ale	11	Claret Punch	47
Brandy and Gum	12	Cocktail, Coffee	82
Brandy Cocktail	18	Cocktail, Saratoga	83
Brandy Crusta	23	Cold Ruby Punch	76
Brandy Daisy	24	Columbia Skin	60

CONTENTS.

	PAGE.
Continental Sour	65
Cordial Lemonade	37
Cosmopolitan Claret Punch	47
Couperee	90
Crimean Cup a la Marmora	91
Curaçoa	96
Curaçoa Punch	47
Currant Shrub	93
Eagle Punch	74
East India Cocktail	19
Egg Milk Punch	48
Egg Nog, Plain	26
Egg Sour	65
El Dorado Punch	48
Empire Punch	81
English Bishop	74
English Royal Punch	80
Faivre's Pousse Café	43
Fancy Brandy Cocktail, No. 1	19
Fancy Brandy Cocktail, No. 2	19
Fancy Gin and Whisky Cocktail	20
Fedora	95
Fine Lemonade for parties	84
Fishing Punch	78
Frapped Café Royal	96
General Jackson Egg Nog	25
Gin and Calamus	32
Gin and Milk	32
Gin and Molasses	33
Gin and Pine	33
Gin and Tansy	33
Gin Cocktail	20
Gin Crusta	23
Gin Daisy	24
Gin Fix	27
Gin Fizz	28
Gin Flip	31
Gin Julep	35
Gin Punch	48
Gin Sangaree	58
Gin Sling	61
Gin Smash	63
Gin Sour	65
Gin Straight	67
Gin Toddy	69
Gin and Wormwood	34
Ginger Daisy	25
Glasgow Flip	31
Golden Fizz	29
"Golden Slipper"	34
Grandeur Punch	81

	PAGE.
Gum Syrup	68
Hari-Kari	35
Hock Cobbler	15
Hot Apple Toddy	69
Hot Boland Punch	46
Hot Gin Sling	61
Hot Irish Punch	49
Hot Lemonade	38
Hot Locomotive	41
Hot Milk Punch	50
Hot Rum	56
Hot Scotch Whisky, (a hint)	73
Hot Scotch Whisky Sling	62
Hot Spiced Rum	57
Hot Whisky Punch	55
How to serve a Pony Glass of Brandy	91
Imperial Egg Nog	26
Italian Wine Lemonade	38
Jamaica Rum Sour	66
Japanese Cocktail	20
Jersey Cocktail	20
"Jersey Lily" Pousse Café	43
Jersey Sour	85
John Collins Gin	34
Kirschwasser Punch	49
Knickerbein	37
Knickerbocker	37
Lemonade	39
Lincoln Club Guzzle	74
Lincoln Club Punch	77
Manhattan Club Oyster Cocktail	97
Manhattan Cocktail No. 1	21
Manhattan Cocktail No. 2	21
Martinez Cocktail	21
May Wine Punch	77
Medford Rum Punch	49
Medford Smash	63
Medford Sour	66
Metropolitan Cocktail	21
Milk Punch	50
Milk and Seltzer	89
Mint Julep	36
Mississippi Punch	50
Morning Glory Fizz	29
Morning Cocktail	83
Mulled Claret	14
Mulled Claret with Egg	14
Old Tom Gin Cocktail	22
Orange Lemonade	38
Orchard Punch	51

	PAGE.
Orgeat Lemonade	39
Orgeat Punch	51
Oxford Punch	80
Parisian Pousse Café, No. 1	44
Parisian Pousse Café, No. 2	44
Peach and Honey	42
Philadelphia Boating Punch	51
Pineapple Julep	88
Pineapple Punch	75
Pony Brandy	13
Port Wine Cobbler	16
Port Wine Flip	31
Port Wine Negus	42
Port Wine Punch	52
Port Wine Sangaree	58
Pousse Café, French	43
Pousse Café, L'Amour	44
Punch	78
Punch a la Fork	95
Punch a la Romaine	79
Rhine Wine Cobbler	16
Rhine Wine Lemonade	39
Rhine Wine and Seltzer	56
Rock and Rye Whisky	73
"Rocky Mountain" Cooler	17
Roman Punch	52
Rum Daisy	25
Rum and Sugar	56
Santa Cruz Fix	89
Santa Cruz Rum Daisy	88
Santa Cruz Sour	91
Santinas Pousse Café	45
Saratoga Cocktail	82
Saratoga, or "Sea Breeze" Egg Lemonade	40
Sauterne Cobbler	16
Sauterne Punch	52
Scotch Whisky Skin	60
Seltzer Lemonade	40
Seventh Regiment Punch	53
Shandy Gaff	59
Sherry Cobbler	16
Sherry and Bitters	59
Sherry and Egg	60
Sherry and Ice	60
Sherry Egg Nog, No. 1	26
Sherry Egg Nog, No. 2	26
Sherry Flip	26
Sherry Wine Punch	53

	PAGE.
Sherry Wine Sangaree	59
Silver Fizz	29
Sixty-ninth Regiment Punch	53
Soda Cocktail	22
Soda Lemonade	40
Soda Nectar	41
Soda Negus	93
Saint Charles Punch	54
Saint Croix Crusta	23
Saint Croix Fix	27
Saint Croix Rum Fizz	30
Saint Croix Rum Punch	54
Saint Croix Sour	66
Stone Fence	68
Stone Wall	85
Suydam, A	68
Tip Top Punch	54
Toledo Punch	75
Tom Collins	92
Tom Collins Brandy	13
Tom Gin and Whisky	72
Tom and Jerry, No. 1	70
Tom and Jerry, How to serve No. 1	71
Tom and Jerry, No. 2	71
Tom and Jerry, How to serve No. 2	71
Tom and Jerry, Cold	72
Vanilla Punch	55
Vermouth Cocktail, No. 1	22
Vermouth Cocktail, No. 2	23
Vermouth Frappée	72
Whisky and Cider	88
Whisky Cobbler	17
Whisky Cocktail	22
Whisky Crusta	24
Whisky Daisy	85
Whisky Fix	28
Whisky Fizz	30
Whisky Flip	32
Whisky Julep	36
Whisky Sling (cold)	62
Whisky Smash	63
Whisky Sour	67
Whisky Straight	68
Whisky Toddy	70
White Lion	72
White Lemonade	41

INVALIDS' DRINKS.

	PAGE.		PAGE.
Apple Water	102	Rice Water	98
Barley Water	99	Simple Beverages from Fruits	101
Cinnamon Water	99		
Currant Jelly Water	100	Tamarind Water	99
Flaxseed Tea	100	Toast Water	100
Flaxseed and Licorice Tea	100	White Wine Whey	98
Grape Juice	101	Wine, Lemon, or Vinegar Whey	100
Lime Water	98		
Oatmeal Drink	99		

TEMPERANCE DRINKS.

Draught Lemonade, or Lemon Sherbet	104	Lemonade Powders	104
		Nectar	106
Draught Lemonade, or Lemon Sherbet (a cheaper method)	105	Orangeade	106
		Raspberry, Strawberry, Currant, or Orange Effervescing Draughts	106
Ginger Lemonade	104		
Imperial Drink for Families	105		
Lemonade	103	Sherbet	105
Lemonade (for parties)	103	Soda Nectar	105

NEW AND UP-TO-DATE DRINKS.

Bamboo Cocktail	131	Mamie Taylor	134
Blackthorn Cocktail	132	Marguerite Cocktail	132
Broadway Cocktail	132	Milo Cocktail	131
Coronation Cocktail	131	Rimson Cooler	134
Egg Lemonade	133	Rob Roy Cocktail	133
Frisco	134	Sloe Gin Cocktail	132
Gin Daisy	133	Sloe Gin Rickey	133
Gin Rickey	133	Star Cocktail	132
Horse's Neck	134	Stewart Cocktail	132
Horse's Collar	134	Whiskey Daisy	133
Liberal Cocktail	131	Whiskey Rickey	134
Mamie Gilroy	134		

STUART'S
FANCY DRINKS
AND
HOW TO MIX THEM.

FANCY DRINKS

AND

HOW TO MIX THEM

Absinthe.

(Small bar glass.)

1 wine-glass absinthe.

Allow water to slowly drop into the glass until full.

Never use absinthe in any preparation unless ordered by the customer.

American Style of Mixing Absinthe.

(A large bar glass.)

½ glass of fine ice.

4 or 5 dashes gum syrup.

1 pony absinthe.

2 wine-glasses of water.

Shake the ingredients until the outside of the shaker is covered with ice. Strain into a large bar glass.

French Style of Mixing Absinthe.

(A large bar glass.)

1 pony glass absinthe.

Fill the bowl of your absinthe glass (which has a hole in the center) with fine ice and the balance with water.

Then elevate the bowl and let the contents drip into the glass containing the absinthe, until the color shows a sufficiency.

Pour into a large bar glass. Serve.

Italian Method of Mixing Absinthe.

(A large bar glass.)

1 pony of absinthe.
2 or 3 pieces of ice.
2 or 3 dashes Maraschino.
½ pony of anisette.

Pour ice water into the glass; slowly stir with a spoon and serve.

"Arf and Arf," or Black and Tan.

(A large ale glass.)

This is a common English drink and means half porter and half ale, but in this country we use half old ale and half new.

It is always best to ask the customer how he desires it.

Bishop.

(A large bar glass.)

1 table-spoon sugar.
2 dashes lemon juice.
Half the juice of an orange.
One squirt seltzer water.
¾ glass filled with fine ice.
Fill the balance with Burgundy.
Dash of Jamaica rum.

Stir well. Dress with fruit, and serve with a straw.

Black Stripe.

(A small bar glass.)

1 wine-glass St. Croix rum or Jamaica.
1 table-spoon "New Orleans" molasses.

If called for in summer, stir in about a table-spoon of water and cool with fine ice.

If in the winter, fill the glass with boiling water, grating a little nutmeg on top, and serve.

Blue Blazer.

½ table-spoon sugar, dissolved in a little hot water.
1 wine-glass Scotch whisky.

Set the liquid on fire, and, while blazing, pour 3 or 4 times from one mug into another. This will give the appearance of a stream of liquid fire.

Twist a piece of lemon peel on top with a little grated nutmeg, and serve.

As this preparation requires skill, it is quite requisite that the amateur should practice with cold water at first.

Brandy and Ginger Ale.

(A large bar glass.)

2 or 3 lumps ice.
1 wine-glass brandy.
1 bottle ginger ale.
Mix well together and serve.

The imported ginger is the best to use as it not only mixes better, but gives more satisfaction.

Brandy and Gum.

(Whisky glass.)

1 or 2 dashes gum syrup.
1 or 2 lumps ice.
Place a spoon in the glass, and hand with a bottle of brandy to the customer.

Brandy and Soda or Stone Wall.

(A large bar glass.)

1 wine-glass brandy.
½ glass with fine ice.
Fill up with plain soda.
The above is a pleasing drink for summer.

Brandy, burned, and Peach.

(Small bar glass.)

1 wine-glass brandy.
½ table-spoon sugar.
Burn brandy and sugar together in a dish or saucer.
2 or 3 slices dried peach.
Place the fruit in the glass, pour the burned liquid over it, grate a little nutmeg on top, and serve.
The above is a Southern preparation, and often used in cases of diarrhœa.

Brandy Champerelle, No. 1.

(A sherry wine glass.)

¼ wine-glass Curacoa (red.)
¼ " Chartreuse (yellow.)
¼ " anisette or Maraschino.
¼ " brandy.
2 or 3 drops Angostura bitters.

To be prepared with the same care as in concocting Poussé Café, not allowing the different liquors to run into one another.

Brandy Champerelle.

(A sherry wine-glass.)

⅓ wine-glass brandy.
⅓ do. Maraschino.
⅓ do. Angostura bitters.
Keep colors separate.

Pony Brandy.

(Pony Glass.)

Set before the customer a small bar glass, and another containing ice water.

Fill a pony glass with best brandy, and pour it into the empty glass.

Brandy Scaffa.

(A sherry glass.)

¼ of raspberry syrup.
¼ of Maraschino.
¼ of Chartreuse (green.)
¼ of brandy.
Keep different articles separate as in Crustas.

Tom Collins Brandy.

(A large bar glass.)

5 or 6 dashes gum syrup.
1 or 2 do. Maraschino.
Juice of small lemon.
1 wine glass brandy.
1 or 2 lumps of ice.

Fill up with plain soda. Do not shake if the soda is cold.

Mulled Claret.

(Large bar glass or **mug.**)

3 or 4 lumps sugar.
2 dashes of lemon juice.
4 or 5 whole allspice, bruised.
2   do. cloves, bruised.
¼ teaspoon ground cinnamon.

2 wine glasses claret; place all the above in a dish; let it come to a boil, and boil 2 minutes, stirring all the time; strain and pour into a large hot glass; grate a little nutmeg on top, and serve.

Mulled Claret and Egg.

(A large bar glass.)

1 table-spoon sugar.
1 dash lemon juice.
¼ teaspoon mixed spices.

1½ wine-glass claret; boil the above ingredients together; then beat to a batter the yolks of 2 eggs with a little sugar added; pour the hot wine over the eggs, stirring continually; grate a little nutmeg on top, and serve. You must positively pour the wine over the eggs, not otherwise, as it would spoil.

California Sherry Cobbler.

(A large bar glass.)

½ table-spoon sugar.
1 pony pine apple syrup.
1½ wine glass of California sherry.
Fill glass with fine ice.

Stir well; dress with fruits, and gently pour a little port on top. Serve with a straw.

California Wine Cobbler.

(A large bar glass.)

Fill glass with fine ice.
¾ table-spoon sugar.
Juice of 1 orange.
1½ wine glass California wine.
Stir well; dress with fruit.
Top with port wine. Serve with a straw.

Catawba Cobbler.

(Large bar glass.)

1 tea-spoon sugar, dissolved in
¼ wine-glass water.
2 wine glasses Catawba wine.

Fill glass with fine ice, and dress with fruits. Serve with a straw.

Champagne Cobbler.

(Large bar glass.)

¾ table-spoon sugar.
1 slice orange.
1 piece lemon peel.

Fill ⅓ glass with fine ice, and the balance with wine, dressed with fruits, and serve with a straw.

Never use the shaker to Champagne beverages.

Claret Cobbler.

Same as Catawba, using claret instead.

Hock Cobbler.

Same as Catawba, using Hock wine instead.

Port Wine Cobbler.

(Large bar glass.)

½ table-spoon sugar.
1 pony of orchard syrup.
Fill glass with fine ice.
1¼ wine glass Port wine.
Stir well; dress with fruit and serve.

Rhine Wine Cobbler.

(A large bar glass.)

1½ table-spoon sugar.
1½ wine glass water.
1½ wine glass Rhine wine.
Fill glass with fine ice; stir well; ornament with fruits, and serve with a straw.

Sauterne Cobbler.

1 tea-spoon sugar.
½ Wine glass orchard syrup.
Fill glass with fine ice.
2 wine glasses Sauterne.
Stir well; dress with fruit, &c.
Serve with straw.

Sherry Cobbler.

(A large bar glass.)

1 table-spoon of sugar.
2 or three slices of orange.
Fill glass with fine ice, then fill up with sherry; shake well and dress top with fruit tastily. Serve with a straw.

Whisky Cobbler.

(A large bar glass.)

2 wine-glasses whisky.
½ table-spoon sugar, dissolved well.
1½ table-spoon pineapple syrup.

Fill glass with fine ice, stir well and dress with fruits; serve with a straw.

Brunswick Cooler.

(A large bar glass.)

Juice of 1 lemon.
½ table-spoon powdered sugar.
1 bottle cold ginger ale.
Stir well; dress with fruit, and serve.

Rocky Mountain Cooler.

1 egg beaten up.
½ table-spoon powdered sugar.
Juice of 1 small lemon.

Add cider, stir well, grate a little nutmeg on top if desired.

Absinthe Cocktail.

(Large bar glass.)

Fill tumbler with ice.
3 or 4 dashes gum syrup.
1 dash Angostura bitters.
1 dash anisette.
½ wine glass water.
½ " " absinthe.

Stir well, strain into a fancy cocktail glass. Twist a piece of lemon peel on top, serve.

Amaranth Cocktail.

Make a regular cocktail and strain into a whisky glass. Fill up with Seltzer or Vichy water. Dip a small spoon in fine sugar, and with what sugar remains upon the spoon, stir up the cocktail, so as to cause it to ferment; have the spoon a little wet, when dipping in the sugar.

Apple Jack Cocktail.

(A large bar glass.)

2 or 3 dashes gum syrup.
2 or 3 dashes raspberry syrup.
1 wine glass apple jack.
Fill glass half full of fine ice.
Shake well; strain into a cocktail glass; twist a bit of lemon peel in it, and serve.

Brandy Cocktail.

(A large bar glass.)

2 or 3 dashes gum syrup.
2 or 3 dashes Angostura or Boker's bitters.
1 or 2 dashes Curacoa.
1 wine glass brandy.
½ the glass fine ice; stir well and strain into a cocktail glass. Twist a piece of lemon peel in to extract the oil, and serve.

Champagne Cocktail.

(Use a champagne goblet.)

Fill one third of the goblet with broken ice.
1 lump of sugar.
1 or 2 dashes Angostura bitters.
1 or 2 slices of orange.

Fill up with wine, and stir.
Serve with a piece of twisted lemon peel on top.
We use none but Boker's, or the genuine Angostura bitters; the latter possesses a certain rich flavor and delicate perfume, altogether unapproachable by others.

East India Cocktail.

(A large bar glass.)

1 tea-spoon raspberry syrup.
1 tea-spoon Curacoa, (red.)
2 or 3 dashes Angostura bitters.
2 or 3 dashes Maraschino.
1 wine glass brandy.
Stir well; strain into a cocktail glass. Twisting a piece of lemon peel on top, serve.

Fancy Brandy Cocktail, No. 1.

(A large bar glass.)

Fill your glass ¾ full of fine ice.
2 or 3 dashes gum syrup.
2 dashes Angostura bitters.
1 or 2 dashes Curacoa.
1 wine glass brandy.
Stir well with a spoon.
Strain into a fancy cocktail glass. Twist a piece of lemon peel on top, and serve.

A squirt of champagne, if kept on draft, will add to the delicacy of flavor.

Fancy Brandy Cocktail, No. 2.

(A large bar glass.)

2 or 3 dashes gum syrup.
2 dashes Maraschino.

2 dashes Angostura bitters.
1 wine-glass brandy.

Twist a piece of lemon peel in the mixture, expressing the oil.

Fill glass half full of fine ice; shake well, and strain into a fancy cocktail glass the rim of which has been moistened with lemon juice.

Fancy Gin and Whisky Cocktails.

Prepared the same as the Brandy No. 2, substituting their respective liquors for brandy.

Gin Cocktail.

(A large bar glass.)

2 or 3 dashes gum syrup.
2 dashes Angostura bitters.
1 wine glass gin.
1 or 2 dashes Curacoa, or absinthe, as the customer prefers.

Fill the glass with fine ice, stir up well; strain into a cocktail glass; squeeze a piece of lemon peel on top, and serve.

Japanese Cocktail.

1 table-spoon orgeat syrup.
1 or 2 dashes Angostura bitters,
1 wine glass brandy.
Fill glass half full fine ice.
Stir well, strain and serve.

Jersey Cocktail.

(A large bar glass.)

½ table-spoon sugar.
4 or 5 pieces ice.

2 or 3 dashes bitters (Angostura).
Fill up with cider.
Twist a piece of lemon peel on top, or use only 1 wine-glass of cider, and strain into a cocktail glass.

Manhattan Cocktail, No. 1.

(A small wine-glass.)

1 pony French vermouth.
½ pony whisky.
3 or 4 dashes Angostura bitters.
3 dashes gum syrup.

Manhattan Cocktail, No. 2.

2 dashes Curacoa.
2 " Angostura bitters.
½ wine-glass whisky.
½ " Italian vermouth.
Fine ice ; stir well and strain into a cocktail glass.

Martinez Cocktail.

Same as Manhattan, only you substitute gin for whisky.

Metropolitan Cocktail.

(A small wine-glass.)

½ pony brandy.
1 " French vermouth.
3 dashes Angostura bitters.
3 " gum syrup.

Old Tom Gin Cocktail.

(A large bar glass.)

Fill glass with fine ice.
2 or 3 dashes gum syrup.
1 or 2 " Angostura bitters.
1 or 2 " Curacoa.
1 wine-glass Old Tom gin.
Stir well.- Strain. Twist a piece of lemon peel on top. Serve.

Soda Cocktail.

(Large bar glass.)

1 tea-spoon sugar.
2 or 3 dashes bitters (Angostura).
5 or 6 lumps of ice.
Fill glass with a bottle of Lemon Soda. Stir well and serve.

You may put a slice of orange on top and berries.

Whisky Cocktail.

(A large bar glass.)

¾ glass fine ice.
2 or 3 dashes gum syrup.
1 or 2 " Angostura bitters.
1 or 2 " Curacoa.
1 wine-glass whisky.
Stir well. Strain into cocktail glass. Twist a piece of lemon peel on top and serve.

Vermouth Cocktail, No. 1.

(A small glass.)

1½ pony French vermouth.
3 dashes Angostura bitters.
2 " gum syrup.

Vermouth Cocktail, No. 2.

(Large bar glass.)

¾ glass filled with fine ice.
4 to 5 dashes gum syrup.
1 or 2   "   Angostura bitters.
2 dashes Maraschino.
1 wine-glass vermouth.

Stir well. Strain into a cocktail glass. A piece of lemon peel on top. Serve.

Brandy Crusta.

(A large bar glass.)

¾ of glass filled with fine ice.
3 or 4 dashes gum syrup.
1 or 2   "   Angostura bitters.
1 or 2   "   lemon juice.
2 dashes Maraschino.
1 wine-glass of brandy.

Procure a nice bright lemon the size of your wine-glass. Peel the rind from it all in one piece; fit it into the glass, covering the entire inside; run a slice of lemon around the edge, and dip the glass in powdered sugar. Strain the mixture after being stirred well into this prepared glass. Dress with a little fruit and serve.

Gin Crusta.

Is prepared same as the Brandy Crusta, substituting Gin for Brandy.

St. Croix Crusta.

(A large bar glass.)

Prepare the rind of a lemon as in a Brandy Crusta, etc.

3 or 4 dashes Orchard syrup.
1 dash of Angostura bitters.
1 " " lemon juice.
2 " " Maraschino.
1 wine-glass of St. Croix rum.
¼ glass fine ice. Stir and strain into the wine-glass. Dress with bits of fruit, berries, and serve.

Whisky Crusta.

(A large bar glass.)

3 or 4 dashes gum syrup.
1 or 2 " Angostura bitters.
1 or 2 " lemon juice.
2 dashes Maraschino.
Fill glass half full of fine ice.
¾ wine-glass whisky.

Mix the ingredients thoroughly. Take a lemon the size of a fancy cocktail glass, peel it so as to have the rind all in one piece, fit it into the cocktail glass. Moisten the edge of your glass with lemon juice, and dip the edge in powdered sugar, then strain the mixture into your prepared glass and serve.

Brandy Daisy.

(A small bar glass.)

3 or 4 dashes gum syrup.
¼ the juice of a lemon.
2 or 3 dashes orange cordial.
1 wine-glass brandy.

Fill glass half full fine ice, shake thoroughly, strain and fill up with Seltzer water or Apollinaris.

Gin Daisy.

Is prepared in the same manner as the Brandy Daisy, substituting gin for brandy.

Ginger Daisy.

This is prepared the same as Brandy Daisy, substituting ginger ale for either Seltzer water or Apollinaris.

Rum Daisy.

Is prepared in the same manner as Brandy Daisy, substituting rum for brandy.

Whisky Daisy.

Is prepared in the same manner as Brandy Daisy substituting whisky for brandy.

Baltimore Egg Nogg.

(Large bar glass.)

1 yolk of an egg, ¾ table spoon of sugar, add a little nutmeg and ground cinnamon to it and beat it to a cream.
1 half pony brandy.
3 or four lumps of ice.
½ pony Jamaica rum.
1 "   Madeira wine.
Fill glass with milk, shake thoroughly, strain, grate a little nutmeg on top and serve.

General Harrison Egg Nogg.

(Large bar glass.)

3 or 4 small pieces of ice.
1 fresh egg.
1 table-spoon sugar.
Fill with cider, shake well, and strain: serve with a little nutmeg on top.

Imperial Egg Nogg.

(Large bar glass.)

1 table-spoon sugar.
1 fresh egg.
One-third glass of fine ice.
1 wine glass brandy.
½ " Jamaica rum.

Fill up with rich milk. Shake thoroughly, in an "egg nogg" shaker, and strain. Grate a little nutmeg on top if desired. Hot Egg Nogg—use hot milk and omit the ice.

Egg Nogg (Plain.)

1 table-spoon sugar.
1 fresh egg.
⅓ glass fine ice.
1 wine-glass whisky.

Fill up with milk. Shake thoroughly in an "egg nogg" shaker, and strain. Grate a little nutmeg on top and serve.

Sherry Egg Nogg, No. 1.

½ table-spoon sugar.
1 egg.
1 pony-glass brandy.
1 wine-glass sherry.

Fill up with fine ice. Shake well. Strain into a fancy bar glass. Serve with nutmeg on top.

Sherry Egg Nogg, No. 2.

(Large bar glass.)

1 table spoon sugar.
1 egg.
2 wine-glasses sherry.

⅓ glass fine ice, fill with milk, shake thoroughly, nutmeg on top.

Apple Jack Fix.

(Large bar glass.)

Same as Brandy Fix, using apple jack instead.

Brandy Fix.

(A large bar glass.)

Fill glass with fine ice.
½ table-spoon sugar dissolved in half wine-glass Seltzer water.
½ pony glass pineapple syrup.
1 wine-glass brandy.
Stir with a spoon. Dress with fruits. Serve with a straw.

Gin Fix.

(A large bar glass.)

½ table-spoon sugar in a little Seltzer.
½ pony pineapple syrup.
Fill glass with fine ice. 1 wine-glass of Holland gin
Stir well. Dress with fruits and serve with a straw.

St. Croix Fix.

(A large bar glass.)

Fill glass with fine ice.
½ table-spoon sugar.
½ wine-glass Seltzer.
2 or three dashes lemon juice.
½ pony pine apple syrup.
1 wine-glass St. Croix rum.
Stir well. Dress with fruit. Serve with a straw.

Whisky Fix.

(A large bar glass.)

½ glass fine ice.
½ table-spoon sugar:
2 or three dashes lemon juice.
½ pony pine apple syrup.
1 wine-glass whisky.

Stir well and dress with fruit. Serve with a straw.

Brandy Fizz.

(A large bar glass.)

½ tea-spoon fine sugar.
Juice of half a lemon.
1 wine-glass brandy.
1 or 2 dashes of white of egg.
½ glass fine ice. Shake well.

Strain into a fizz glass; fill up with seltzer or Vichy. This must be imbibed immediately.

Gin Fizz.

(A large bar glass.)

½ table-spoon sugar.
3 or four dashes lemon juice.
One wine-glass Old Tom gin.

Put all in the glass, ½ full of fine ice; stir well with a spoon; strain into a fizz glass. Fill up with seltzer or Vichy water and do not fail to drink quickly.

Golden Fizz.

1 egg (yolk only.)
1 table-spoon sugar.
2 or 3 dashes lemon juice.
1 wine-glass Old Tom gin or whisky.
¾ of the glass fine ice.
Use the shaker well ; strain into a fizz glass.
Fill up with seltzer or Vichy and drink immediately.

Morning Glory Fizz.

(Large bar glass.)

Fill the glass three-quarters full with fine ice.
Mix 3 or 4 dashes absinthe in a little water.
3 dashes lime juice.
4 or 5 dashes lemon juice.
1 table-spoon sugar.
The white of 1 egg.
A wine-glass of Scotch whisky.

Shake well in a shaker and strain ; fill balance of glass with seltzer or Vichy water.

To be drank immediately, or the effect will be lost. It is a morning beverage, a tonic and a nerve quieter.

Silver Fizz.

(A large bar glass.)

½ table-spoon sugar.
3 or 4 dashes lemon juice.

1 wine-glass "Old Tom" gin.
The white, only, of an egg.
Fill with ice; shake up well; strain into a fizz glass.
Fill the glass with seltzer from a syphon and drink immediately.

St. Croix Rum Fizz.

Is prepared same as Brandy Fizz, simply substituting rum for Brandy.

Whisky Fizz.

½ tea-spoon fine sugar.
Juice of half a lemon.
1 or 2 dashes of the white of egg.
1 wine-glass whisky.
¾ glass-full of fine ice.

Shake well; strain into a fizz glass; fill it with seltzer water or Vichy. Serve.

Brandy Flip.

(Large bar glass.)

½ fill glass with fine ice.
1 egg beaten thoroughly.
½ table-spoon sugar.
1 wine-glass brandy.

Use the shaker in mixing; strain into a fancy bar glass; grate a little nutmeg on top; serve.

Gin Flip.

(A large bar glass.)

1 table-spoon sugar dissolved in a little seltzer water.
1 wine-glass Holland gin.

Fill glass half full fine ice ; shake well, and strain into a fancy glass and serve.

Glasgow Flip.

Beat 1 egg thoroughly.
Add the juice of 1 lemon.
½ table-spoon powdered sugar.
Balance cold ginger ale.
 tir well and serve.

Port Wine Flip.

(A large bar glass.)

1 egg.
1 table-spoon sugar.
¾ glass of fine ice.
1 wine-glass port wine.

Use a shaker in mixing.
Strain into a wine-glass.
Grate a little nutmeg on top. Serve.

Sherry Flip.

(A large bar glass.)

½ the glass fine ice.
1 egg.
½ table-spoon sugar.
1½ wine-glass sherry.

Shake well; strain into a fancy glass with nutmeg on top. Serve.

Whisky Flip.

Is prepared same as Brandy Flip, substituting whisky for brandy.

Gin and Calamus.

(A whisky glass.)

Steep 2 or 3 pieces calamus root, cut in small bits in a bottle of gin until the essence is extracted.

To serve, you simply hand out the glass together with the bottle, allowing the customer to help himself.

Gin and Milk.

(A whisky glass.)

Put out a glass and bar spoon with the bottle of gin, allowing the customer to help himself, after he has done so, fill up the glass with iced-cold milk.

Gin and Molasses.

(A whisky glass.)

Cover the bottom of the glass with a little gin. Drop in 1 table-spoon of New Orleans molasses, then place the bottle of gin to the customer, allowing him to help himself. After dropping in the molasses, put a small bar spoon in the glass.

Hot water must be used to clean the glass afterwards.

Gin and Pine.

Take some fine slivers of pine wood from the center of a green pine log, steep them in a bottle of gin to extract the flavor; in about two hours the gin will be ready to serve, which is done in same manner as dispensing gin and tansy.

Gin and Tansy.

(A whisky glass.)

This is an old-fashioned but excellent tonic, and is prepared by steeping a bunch of tansy in a bottle of Holland gin, which extracts the essence.

In serving, you simply set the glass, with a lump of ice dropped into it, before the customer, allowing him to help himself from the bottle containing the preparation.

Gin and Wormwood.

(A small bar glass.)

5 or 6 sprigs of wormwood placed in a quart bottle of gin to extract the essence. Place before the customer a small bar glass (dropping a piece of ice therein), and the bottle, allowing him to help himself. This is a very old drink, used principally in country villages.

John Collins' Gin.

(Extra large bar glass.)

1 table-spoon sugar.
About 5 dashes lemon juice.
1 wine-glass gin.
5 or 6 small bits of ice.
1 bottle plain soda.
Mix well, remove the ice, and serve.

Golden Slipper.

(A wine glass.)

½ wine-glass Chartreuse (yellow.)
1 yolk of an egg.
½ wine-glass Danziger goldwasser.
This is a favorite with American ladies, much relished.
Be careful when preparing this beverage not to disturb the yolk of the egg.

Hari-Kari.

Make a whisky sour large enough to half fill a brandy glass or tumbler when strained, and fill with seltzer or Vichy to suit the party.

Dress with fruits in season.

Brandy Julep.

Is made same as the Mint Julep, omitting the fancy fixings, however.

Champagne Julep.

(A large bar glass.)

1 lump of white sugar.
1 sprig mint, press to extract the essence.

Pour the wine into the glass slowly, stirring gently continually.

Dress with sliced orange, grapes and berries, tastily, and serve.

Gin Julep.

(A large bar glass.)

Fill with fine ice.
¾ table-spoon sugar.
½ wine-glass water.

3 or 4 sprigs mint, pressed as in Mint Julep, to extract the essence.

1¼ wine-glass Holland gin.

Stir well, and dress with fruits in season, and serve.

Mint Julep.

(Large bar glass.)

1 table-spoon sugar dissolved in ½ wine-glass water.

3 or 4 sprigs mint, which you press well in the sugar and water to extract the flavor, then add 1½ wine-glass brandy, after which withdraw the mint and stir the ingredients well ; then fill glass with fine ice and insert the mint again, stems downward, leaves above. Dress tastily with fruits in season.

Give a dash of Jamaica rum, a sprinkle of white sugar, and serve with a straw placed across top of glass.

Whisky Julep.

(A large bar glass.)

¾ tablespoon sugar dissolved in ½ wine-glass water.

3 or 4 sprigs mint, press to extract the essence.

1 wine-glass whisky.

A dash of Jamaica rum.

Stir well with spoon ; arrange the mint with stems downward.

Dress with pineapple, oranges, and berries, tastily ; some omit the fruit.

Serve with a straw.

CORDIAL LEMONADE.

Knickerbein.

(A sherry wine-glass.)

⅔ of a wine-glass of vanilla cordial.
1 yolk of egg, which carefully cover with benedictine.
¹/₃ wine-glass of Kümmel.
2 drops Angostura or Boker's bitters.

The same rule is here applied as in making Poussé Café, viz. : Keep colors separate and the different portions from running into each other.

Knickerbocker.

(Large bar glass.)

2 table-spoons raspberry syrup.
Juice of half a lemon.
A slice of pineapple and orange.
1 wine-glass St. Croix rum.
½ wine-glass Curacoa.

Fill glass with fine ice ; stir well, adding fruit in season, and imbibe through a straw.

Cordial Lemonade.

Make a plain lemonade; ornament with fruits in season; then put in slowly ½ a pony of any cordial.

Hot Lemonade.

(A large bar glass.)

1 table-spoon sugar; ½ a lemon squeezed well; fill the glass with hot water; stir well, and serve.

Pour a little hot water into the glass, and shake around it before making the drink to prevent the glass from cracking.

Italian Wine Lemonade.

(A large bar glass.)

1 table spoon sugar, dissolved in a little water.
4 or 5 dashes lemon juice.
¾ glass filled with fine ice.
1 wine-glass sherry, claret, or Port wine.

Fill up with water; stir well; dress top with fruits, and serve with a straw.

Orange Lemonade.

(A large bar glass.)

¾ glass fine ice.
1 table-spoon sugar.
Juice of 1 orange.
1 or 2 dashes lemon juice.

Fill up with water; shake and dress with fruit. Serve with a straw.

Orgeat Lemonade.

½ table-spoon sugar.
4 or 5 dashes lemon juice.
1½ wine-glass orgeat.
¾ glass fine ice.

Fill glass up with water; stir well; dress with fruit and serve with a straw.

Lemonade.

(Large bar glass.)

1½ table-spoon sugar.
Juice of ½ a lemon.

Fill ¾ with fine ice; balance with water; shake well; serve.

Some add a tablespoon of raspberry or strawberry syrup, dashing with Port wine, and dressing with fruit.

Lemonade.

Slice very thin 3 lemons, to which add ½ lb. of white lump sugar; mix well together, and throw in one gallon water.

Rhine Wine Lemonade.

(Prepare in a goblet.)

1 table-spoon sugar.
Juice of ½ a lemon.

A little ice, and fill up with Rhine wine; dress with fruit in season, and serve.

Saratoga or Sea Breeze Egg Lemonade.

(A large bar glass.)

1 egg.
1 table-spoon sugar.
½ the juice of a lemon.

Fill ¾ of the glass with fine ice; balance with water; use the shaker until well mixed; strain and serve; grate a little nutmeg on top.

Seltzer Lemonade.

(Large bar glass.)

1½ table-spoon sugar.
5 or 6 dashes lemon juice.
½ doz. bits of ice.

Fill up with Seltzer water.
Stir well and serve.

Soda Lemonade.

(A large bar glass.)

1 tablespoon sugar.
3 or four lumps of ice.
3 or 4 dashes lemon juice.
1 bottle plain soda water.
Stir well; remove the ice. Serve.

Wine Lemonade.

(A large bar glass.)

Fill glass with fine ice.
3 or 4 dashes lemon juice.
1 table-spoon sugar.
1 wine-glass of whatever kind of wine is desired.
Fill up with water; shake well; dress with fruits. Serve with straw.

Hot Locomotive.

(A large bar glass.)

1 yolk of egg.
½ table-spoon sugar, and 1 pony honey, mixed well together.
½ pony Curacoa.
1½ wine-glass Burgundy or claret boiled; mix all thoroughly together; place a thin slice of lemon on top, with a sprinkle of cinnamon, and serve.

Soda Nectar.

(A large bar glass.)

The juice of 1 lemon.
½ glass of Seltzer water.
White sugar to taste.
½ a small tea spoon of bi-carbonate of soda.

Mix the lemon, water and sugar together thoroughly, then put in the bi-carbonate of soda, stir well, and drink while it is foaming. This is a very pleasant beverage for a morning drink, and a gentle purge for the bowels.

Peach and Honey.

(A small bar glass.)

1 table-spoon honey.
1 wine-glass peach brandy; stir well with a spoon; serve.
This is a favorite with many.

Port Wine Negus.

(A small bar glass.)

1 tea-spoon sugar.
1 wine glass Port wine.
Fill glass ½ full of hot water.
Grate a little nutmeg on top. Serve.

American Pousse Cafe.

¼ Maraschino.
¼ Curacoa.
¼ Chartreuse (green).
¼ brandy.
Keep the colors separate.

Faivre's Pousse Cafe.

(A sherry wine-glass.)

1/3 glass Benedictine.
1/3 " Curacoa.
1/3 " Kirschwasser
3 drops bitters.

Be careful and not allow the different colors to mix with each other.

Pousse Cafe, French.

(A sherry wine-glass.)

⅓ glass Maraschino.
1/6 " raspberry syrup.
1/6 " vanilla.
1/6 " Curacoa.
1/6 " Chartreuse.
1/6 " brandy.

In compounding the above, use a small wine-glass for pouring in each article separately, be very careful in doing so, that each portion may be separate. Serve without mixing.

"Jersey Lily" Pousse Cafe.

(Pony glass.)

Half fill with Chartreuse.
Half " " brandy.

Pour brandy in carefully, so as not to disturb the Chartreuse, and serve.

Pousse L'Amour.

(A sherry wine-glass.)

½ glass Maraschino.
The yolk of 1 egg carefully.
Then add ¼ glass vanilla cordial.
¼ glass of brandy.
Serve without mixing. Be careful and see that the colors do not run into each other.

Parisian Pousse Cafe, No. 1.

(A sherry wine glass.)

5 drops raspberry syrup.
¼ of the glass Maraschino.
¼ " " Curacoa.
¼ " " Chartreuse.
¼ " " brandy.
Keep the five colors separate and serve without mixing.

Parisian Pousse Cafe, No. 2.

⅕ glass Maraschino.
$2/5$ Kirschwasser.
$1/5$ Chartreuse.
Brandy on top.

Santinas New Orleans Pousse Cafe.

(A sherry wine-glass.)

⅓ wine-glass brandy.
⅓ " Maraschino.
⅓ " Curacoa.

Careful attention must be paid to the arrangement of colors, and to preventing the different portions from running into each other.

Arrack Punch.

(A bar glass.)

1 table-spoon sugar dissolved in a little water.
1 or 2 dashes lemon juice.
1 wine-glass of Batavia arrack.
¼ fill glass with fine ice. Shake well. Dress with fruits, and serve with a straw.

Hot Arrack Punch.

(A hot water glass.)

1 tea-spoon sugar.
1 or 2 dashes lemon juice.
½ wine-glass arrack.

Fill up with hot water. Stir well; grate a little nutmeg on top, and serve.

Hot Boland Punch.

1 lump sugar.
2 wine-glasses boiling water.
1½ "   Scotch whisky.
1 table-spoon ginger ale.

Brandy Punch.

(A large bar glass.)

1 table-spoon sugar dissolved in a little water.
½ of a small lemon.
¼ wine-glass St. Croix rum.
1½ "   brandy.
1 piece pineapple.
1 or 2 slices orange.

Fill glass with fine ice. Shake well. Dress with fruits and serve with a straw.

Champagne Punch.

(Serve in champagne goblets.)

1 quart bottle wine.
¾ lb. sugar.
1 orange sliced.
The juice of 1 lemon.
3 or 4 slices of pineapple.
1 wine-glass strawberry syrup. Dress with fruit, and serve.

Claret Punch.

(A large bar glass.)

1½ table-spoon sugar.
1 slice lemon.
2 slices orange.
Fill glass with fine ice. Pour in claret wine. Shake well. Dress with fruit in season, and serve with a straw.

Cosmopolitan Claret Punch.

(Use a goblet.)

⅓ filled with chopped ice.
1½ pony brandy.
½ table-spoon sugar.
Fill with claret.
Shake well and dress with berries and fruit, and serve.

Curacoa Punch.

(Large bar glass.)

¾ table-spoon sugar.
3 or 4 dashes lemon juice.
1 wine glass brandy.
1 pony glass Curacoa, (red.)
½ pony glass Jamaica rum; dress with fruits as usual.
Fill with fine ice and sip through a straw.

Egg Milk Punch.

(A large bar glass.)

1 Egg.
¾ table-spoon sugar.
1 wine-glass brandy.
1 pony-glass St. Croix rum.
½ glass with fine ice.
Fill up with milk—use the shaker in mixing—which must be done thoroughly to a cream.

Strain; grate a little nutmeg on top, and it is ready.

El Dorado Punch.

1 table-spoon sugar.
1 pony-glass brandy.
½ pony-glass Jamaica rum.
½ pony-glass Bourbon whisky.
1 slice of lemon.
Fill glass with fine ice; shake thoroughly. Dress with fruit, and serve with a straw.

Gin Punch.

(A large bar glass.)

2 table-spoons white sugar.
1 pony Seltzer.
1½ wine glass Holland gin, 4 or 5 dashes lemon juice.
Fill glass with fine ice.
Shake well. Dress with 2 slices orange; one half slice pineapple, and berries; serve with a straw.

Hot Irish Punch.

(A hot water glass.)

1 or 2 lumps sugar.
1 or 2 dashes of lemon juice.
1 wine-glass Irish whisky.
Fill up with hot water; stir well.
Place a slice of lemon on top, grate a little nutmeg, and serve.

Kirschwasser Punch.

(A large bar glass.)

½ table-spoon sugar.
2 or 3 dashes lemon juice.
3 or 4 dashes Chartreuse.
1 wine-glass Kirschwasser.
Fill ¾ of the glass with fine ice.
Dress with fruits; serve with a straw.

Medford Rum Punch.

(A large bar glass.)

Fill glass with fine ice.
½ table-spoon sugar.
2 or 3 dashes lemon juice.
1½ glass Medford rum.
1 dash of Jamaica rum.
Stir well. Dress with fruits. Serve with straw.

Milk Punch.

(A large bar glass.)

One-third glass fine ice.
¾ table-spoon sugar.
1 wine-glass brandy.
1 wine-glass St. Croix rum.
½ wine-glass Jamaica rum.

Fill up with fresh milk, mix well together, strain, and serve up, with a little nutmeg on top.

Hot Milk Punch.

(A large bar glass.)

1 table-spoon of sugar.
½ wine-glass St. Croix rum.
½ wine-glass brandy.
Fill the glass with hot milk.

Mix well with a spoon; grate nutmeg on top, and serve. **Always mix with a spoon. Never use the shaker to this.**

Mississippi Punch.

(Large bar glass.)

1 table-spoon sugar, dissolved in ½ wine-glass water.
2 or 3 dashes lemon juice.
½ wine-glass Bourbon whisky.
½ wine-glass Jamaica rum.
1 wine-glass brandy.

Fill goblet with fine ice; dress top with pieces orange, pine apple, &c.

Orchard Punch.

(A large bar glass.)

2 table-spoons orchard syrup.
2 or 3 dashes of lime or lemon juice.
½ pony pineapple syrup.
Fill glass with fine ice.
1 wine-glass California brandy.
Stir well. Dress with fruits, dash with a little Port wine, and serve with a straw.

Orgeat Punch.

(A large bar glass.)

1½ table-spoon orgeat syrup.
1½ wine-glass brandy.
4 or 5 dashes lemon.
Fill glass with fine ice.
Shake well. Dress with fruits; top off with a dash of Port wine. Serve with straw.

Philadelphia Boating Punch.

(A large bar glass.)

Fill glass with fine ice.
1 table-spoon sugar.
1 or 2 dashes lemon juice.

1 wine glass St. Croix rum.
1 pony of old brandy.
Stir well. Dress with fruits, and serve with a straw.

Port Wine Punch.

(A large bar glass.)

½ table-spoon sugar.
½ table spoon orchard syrup.
1 or 2 dashes lemon juice,
1½ wine-glass Port wine.
Fill up with fine ice, stir well, and dress top with fruits in season. Serve with a straw.

Roman Punch.

(A large bar glass.)

½ fill glass with fine ice.
1 table-spoon sugar.
2 or 3 dashes lemon juice.
Juice of half an orange.
½ pony Curacoa.
½ wine-glass brandy.
½ pony " Jamaica Rum.
Stir well. Dash with port wine. Dress with fruit. Serve with straw.

Sauterne Punch.

Is composed of the same ingredients as Claret Punch, but substituting Sauterne wine for claret.

7th Regiment Punch.

(A large bar glass.)

1 table-spoon sugar.
2 or 3 dashes lemon juice.
1 wine-glass brandy.
1 wine-glass Catawba wine.

Flavor with raspberry syrup. Fill glass with fine ice; shake well. Dress with fruits. Dash with Jamaica rum and serve with a straw.

Sherry Wine Punch.

(A large bar glass.)

Fill glass with fine ice.
2 wine-glasses sherry.
1 table-spoon sugar.
2 or 3 dashes lemon juice.

Stir well. Dress with fruits and top off with a little claret. Serve with a straw.

69th Regiment Punch.

(A hot whisky glass.)

½ wine-glass Irish whisky.
½ "   Scotch "
1 tea-spoon sugar.
2 or 3 dashes lemon juice.

2 wine-glasses hot water.

The imbibition of the above adds greatly to one's comfort on a cold night.

St. Charles Punch.

(Large bar glass.)

1 table-spoon sugar.
¼ of lemon juice.
1 wine-glass port wine.
1 pony glass brandy.
1 wine-glass Port wine.

Fill with fine ice. Shake well. Dress top with fruits in season and serve with straw.

St. Croix Rum Punch.

(Large bar glass.)

1 table-spoon sugar.
3 or 4 dashes lemon juice.
¼ pony-glass Jamaica rum.
1 wine-glass St. Croix rum.

Fill up with fine ice. Dress top with fruit and berries. Serve with a straw.

Tip Top Punch.

(A large bar glass.)

3 or four lumps of ice.
1 pony of brandy.

1 lump of sugar.
2 slices pineapple.
2 slices orange.
1 or 2 dashes lemon juice.
Fill with champagne. Stir well. Dress with fruits
Serve with a straw.

Vanilla Punch.

1 table-spoon sugar dissolved in a little water.
3 or 4 dashes lemon juice.
2 or 3 dashes Curacoa.
1 wine-glass brandy.
1 pony-glass Vanilla cordial.
Fill with fine ice. Mix well. Dress tastily with berries and fruit in season and serve with a straw. Or you can flavor with a little Vanilla extract instead of the cordial.

Hot Whisky Punch.

(A hot whisky glass.)

The juice of half a lemon, one or two lumps of sugar dissolved in one wine-glass hot water.

2 wine-glasses Scotch or Irish whisky.

Fill glass with boiling water and place on top a thin slice of lemon or a piece of the peel. Some grate a little nutmeg on top. Always place ice before the customer, and allow a spoon to remain in the drink, in order that the partaker of the beverage can help himself to ice should the mixture be too hot for him.

Rhine Wine and Seltzer.

(A large bar glass.)

Fill glass half full Rhine wine, balance with Seltzer. Both the Rhine wine and Seltzer should be kept on ice. The above is a favorite drink among the Germans, who prefer it to lemonade.

Rum and Sugar.

(A whisky glass.)

1 or 2 dashes gum syrup.
1 lump of ice.
1 wine-glass Jamaica rum.

Stir well and serve—or fix glass with syrup and ice as above, leaving a small spoon in the glass. Set it and the bottle before the customer, allowing him to help himself.

Hot Rum.

(A hot water glass.)

1 tea-spoon sugar.
A small lump of butter.
1 wine-glass Jamaica rum.

Fill glass with hot water. Stir well and serve. Omit spices.

Hot Spiced Rum.

(Hot water glass.)

1 tea-spoon sugar.
1 tea-spoon of mixed whole allspice and cloves, and a piece of butter about the size of a small marble.
1 wine-glass Jamaica Rum.

Fill glass with hot water. Mix well and serve.

Ale Sangaree.

(An ale glass.)

1 tea-spoon powdered sugar.

Fill up with ale, grate nutmeg on top, and serve.

Brandy Sangaree.

(Small bar glass.)

2 small lumps of ice.
½ wine-glass water.
1 " brandy.
1 tea-spoon sugar.

Stir well ; give a dash of Port wine on top, and serve.

Gin Sangaree.

⅓ tea-spoon sugar dissolved in a little water.
1 wine-glass Holland gin.
1 lump of ice.

Stir with a spoon ; put about a tea-spoon of sherry on top, and serve.

Porter Sangaree.

(A large bar glass.)

½ table-spoon sugar.
3 or 4 lumps of ice.
Fill up with porter.

Stir well ; remove the ice ; grate nutmeg on top, and serve.

Port Wine Sangaree.

(A small bar glass.)

1 or 2 lumps ice.
1 tea-spoon sugar.
1½ wine-glass Port wine.

Shake well ; remove ice ; grate a little nutmeg on top serve.

Sherry Wine Sangaree.

(A whisky glass.)

1 tea-spoon sugar.
1 or 2 lumps of ice.
1 wine-glass sherry.

Shake well; remove ice, grate a little nutmeg on top, and serve.

Shandy Gaff.

(Large bar glass.)

Half the glass fill with lager.
" " " " " ginger ale.

It is also made with half ale and half ginger ale.

Sherry and Bitters.

(A sherry wine-glass.)

1 dash Angostura bitters.
1 wine-glass sherry.

To prepare the above artistically, dash in your bitters, then twist the glass in a way to cover the inside; fill up with sherry, and serve.

Sherry and Egg.

(A whisky glass.)

1 egg, ice cold.
1 wine-glass sherry wine.
Before dropping in the egg, cover the bottom of the glass with a little sherry, this will prevent the egg adhering to the glass, or, after preparing the egg as above, set the bottle of sherry before the customer and allow him to help himself.

Sherry and Ice.

(A whisky glass.)

1 or 2 lumps of ice and a small bar spoon in the glass, hand this to the customer with the bottle of sherry, allowing him to help himself.

Columbia Skin.

(Small whisky glass.)

Prepare this the same as a Whisky Skin, which it is, but is called in Boston by the above name.

Scotch Whisky Skin.

(A small whisky glass.)

1 wine-glass Scotch whisky.
Fill glass half full with hot water, put a piece of lemon peel on top, and serve.

Brandy Sling.

(A hot-water glass.)

1 lump sugar.
1 wine-glass brandy.

Fill up with hot water; stir well; grate nutmeg on top; serve.

For a cold Brandy Sling, use a lump of ice and cold water.

Gin Sling.

1 lump of sugar dissolved in a little water.
1 lump of ice.
1 wine-glass gin.

Stir, and grate a little nutmeg on top.

Hot Gin Sling.

(A hot water glass.)

1 tea-spoon sugar.
1 wine-glass Holland gin.

Fill up with hot water; stir well; grate a little nutmeg on top, and serve.

Whisky Sling (cold).

(Small bar glass.)

1 tea-spoon sugar dissolved in half wine-glass water.
1 or 2 small lumps of ice.
1 wine-glass whisky.

Stir well, and grate nutmeg on top, and serve.

Hot Scotch Whisky Sling.

(Hot water glass.)

A wine-glass Scotch whisky.
A lump of sugar.
A piece of lemon peel.

Fill glass ¾ full with boiling water; grate nutmeg on top, and serve.

Brandy Smash.

(Large bar glass.)

½ table-spoon sugar.
½ wine-glass water.
2 or 3 sprigs mint, pressed as in mint julep.
1 wine-glass brandy.

Fill glass ½ full fine ice.
Stir well; strain into a fancy bar glass, and serve.

Gin Smash.

(Large bar glass.)

½ the glass fine ice.
½ table-spoon sugar.
2 or 3 sprigs mint, pressed as in mint julep.
1 wine-glass Holland gin.

Stir well; strain into a sour glass; dress with fruit; serve.

Medford Rum Smash.

(Large bar glass.)

½ tablespoon sugar, dissolved in a little water.
2 or 3 sprigs mint, pressed to extract the essence
½ glass fine ice.
1 wine-glass Medford rum.

Stir well; strain; dress with fruit; replacing mint leaves upward, and serve.

Whisky Smash.

(Large bar glass.)

½ table-spoon sugar.
2 or 3 sprigs mint, pressed to extract essence, as in a julep.
½ glass with fine ice.
1 wine-glass whisky.

Stir well; strain into a fancy or sour glass; dress with a little fruit, berries, &c. Serve.

Apple Jack Sour.

(A large bar glass.)

Fill glass ¾ full fine ice.
½ table-spoon sugar in a little water.
2 or 3 dashes lemon juice.
1 wine-glass old apple jack.
Stir well; strain into a sour glass; dress with fruit, and serve.

Brandy Sour.

(A large bar glass.)

Fill glass with ice.
½ table-spoon sugar.
2 or 3 dashes lemon juice.
A squirt of Seltzer.
1 wine-glass brandy.
Stir well; strain into a sour glass; dress with fruits as usual, and serve.

Champagne Sour.

(Large bar glass.)

1 tea-spoon sugar.
2 or 3 dashes lemon juice.

One-third fine ice.

Fill up with wine; stir well, and dress with fruit and berries in season.

Continental Sour.

½ tea-spoon sugar, dissolved in water.
Juice of ½ a lemon.
1 wine-glass whisky or liquor as desired; fine ice; shake well, and strain into a sour glass, and dash with claret.

Egg Sour.

1 table-spoon powdered sugar.
3 lumps of ice.
1 egg.
Juice of 1 lemon.
Shake thoroughly; serve with straw; **nutmeg grated on top.**

Gin Sour.

(A small bar glass.)

½ table-spoon sugar.
4 or 5 dashes lemon juice.
1 squirt Seltzer water.
½ glass fine ice.
1 wine-glass Holland gin.

Stir well; strain into a sour glass; **dress with a little fruit, and serve.**

Jamaica Rum Sour.

(Large bar glass.)

¾ of glass fine ice.
½ table-spoon sugar.
2 or 3 dashes lemon juice.
½ wine glass Seltzer.
1   "   Jamaica rum.

Stir well, and strain into a sour glass; dress with fruit, serve.

Medford Rum Sour.

(Large bar glass.)

½ table-spoon sugar.
3 or 4 dashes lemon juice.
1 dash of Seltzer from syphon.
1 wine-glass Medford rum; fill glass half full with ice; strain and dress with fruits.

St. Croix Sour.

(Large bar glass.)

½ table-spoon sugar, dissolved in a little Seltzer water.
¼ of a lemon squeezed into the glass.
½ glass fine ice.

1 wine-glass St. Croix rum.

Stir well; strain into a sour glass; dress with fruit in season, and serve.

Whisky Sour.

(Large bar glass.)

Fill glass with fine ice.
½ table-spoon sugar.
3 or 4 dashes lemon juice.
½ wine-glass Seltzer water.
1 wine-glass whisky.

Stir well; strain into a sour glass; dress with fruit, and serve.

Brandy Straight.

(A whisky glass.)

Drop a small lump of ice in the glass, and hand it with the bottle of brandy to your customer.

Gin Straight.

Same as Brandy Straight, substituting gin instead of brandy.

Whisky Straight.

Same as Brandy Straight, substituting whisky for brandy.

Stone Fence.

(A whisky glass.)

1 wine-glass Bourbon whisky or apple-jack.
2 or 3 lumps of ice.
Fill up with cider. Stir well, and serve.

A Suydam.

1 dash orange bitters.
1 " Angostura bitters.
Then hand the bottle of liquor out and let customer help himself. This is an appetizer.

Gum Syrup.

14 lbs. loaf sugar.
1 gallon water.

Boil together for 5 minutes, and add water to make up 2 gallons.

Plain Syrup.

6½ lbs. loaf sugar.
½ gallon water.
Boil until dissolved, and filter through flannel.

Hot Apple Toddy.

(A hot apple toddy glass.)

½ table-spoon sugar.
½ a baked apple.
1 wine-glass apple-jack.
Fill balance with hot water.
Mix well, using a spoon, grate a little nutmeg on top.
Serve, leaving the spoon in the glass.

Brandy Toddy.

1 tea-spoon sugar dissolved in a little water.
1 wine-glass brandy.
1 lump ice.
Stir with a spoon.
For hot brandy toddy omit the ice and use hot water.

Gin Toddy.

(A whisky glass.)

1 or 2 bits of broken ice.
½ tea-spoon sugar.
1 wine-glass Holland gin.

Stir well, and serve; or you may dissolve the sugar with a little water, put spoon and ice in glass, and hand the bottle to the customer.

Whisky Toddy.

(Small bar glass.)

1 tea-spoon sugar dissolved in water.
A piece of ice.
1 wine-glass whisky.

Stir and serve; or dissolve the sugar in the glass with a little, and set the bottle of whisky before the customer.

Tom and Jerry, No. 1.

(Prepare in a punch bowl.)

The number of eggs to be used in this preparation depends upon the quantity you intend making.

Be very careful in having your eggs fresh.

Separate the yolks from the whites.

Beat the whites to a very stiff froth, and add 1½ table-spoon of white sugar to each egg, mixing thoroughly together. Then beat the yolks until they are thin as liquor, which, mix thoroughly with the whites and sugar until the compound attains the consistency of batter.

To prevent the sugar settling to the bottom of the bowl, put in as much carbonate of soda as will cover a ten-cent piece, or stir once in a while.

TOM AND JERRY, NO. 2.

How to Serve it.

2 table-spoons of the mixture.
1 wine-glass brandy.
1 pony " Jamaica rum.

Fill the mug up with hot water, or hot milk, stirring well with a spoon. Pour from one mug into the other to thoroughly mix, grate a little nutmeg on top, and catch on.

Tom and Jerry No. 2.

(Prepare in a punch bowl.)

Beat the whites of 1 dozen eggs to a stiff froth, and the yolks until they become as thin as water. Mix well together, then add:

½ a small glass Jamaica rum.
¼ "   "   St. Croix rum.
1½ tea-spoon ground cinnamon.
⅓ "   "   cloves.
¼ "   "   allspice.

Stiffen with white sugar to the consistency of batter.

How to Serve the Above: Use a Small Bar Glass or Mug.

1 table-spoon of the mixture.
1 wine-glass brandy.

Fill up with boiling water or milk, a little grated nutmeg on top. Serve.

Cold Tom and Jerry.

For this, use as above, only you add cold water or milk instead of hot.

Tom Collins Gin and Whisky

Are concocted in the same manner as the brandy receipt, substituting their respective liquors.

Vermouth Frappee.

(A large bar glass.)

1½ pony French vermouth.
½ glass filled with shaved ice.
Fill up with cold Seltzer water.

White Lion.

(Large bar glass.)

1 table-spoon sugar, dissolved in water. Squeeze juice from half a lemon, putting the rind in the glass.
2 tea-spoons raspberry syrup.
1 wine-glass St. Croix rum.
½ pony glass Curacoa.

Mix well. Fill with fine ice. Dress with berries, etc. Serve

Rock and Rye Whisky.

(A whisky glass.)

½ table-spoon rock candy syrup.
1 wine-glass rye whisky.

Stir well and serve, or you may drop the syrup into the glass and leaving the spoon in, allow the customer to help himself to the whisky. Procure the pure rock candy syrup and best rye whisky. The above is a most excellent medicament for colds and sore throats.

Hot Scotch Whisky.

(A hint.)

May be improved by adding one or two drops of sherry wine.

Elderberry Beer.

Secure about twenty gallons of the first and strong wort.

Boil ½ bushel of elderberries and when cold strain them into the wort and let it work in the barrel. You will be surprised at the result. At the end of a year you will have an excellent Port wine.

Family Beer.

10 galls. boiling water.
15 oz. ground ginger.
10 oz. cream tartar.
10 lemons sliced.

Put all together and when nearly cool strain and add 15 lbs. brown sugar. After which cut ½ oz. oil of cloves and ¼ oz. oil cinnamon, in 4 oz. alcohol. When luke-warm, put in 1 pint of yeast and in 15 hours skim and filter it. If bottled, tie corks down carefully.

Lincoln Club Guzzle.

1 bottle ginger ale.
1 pony Santa Croix rum.
Mix well.

English Bishop.

(Use a small punch bowl.)

1 quart of the best Port wine.
1 orange (stuck pretty well with cloves.)

Roast the orange before a fire, and when sufficiently brown, cut in quarters, and pour over it the Port wine, (previously made hot), add sugar to taste, and let the mixture simmer over the fire for half an hour.

Eagle Punch:

1 bottle of Islay whisky.
1 bottle of Monongahela
Lemon peel, sugar and—boiling water.

Toledo Punch.

(Use a large punch bowl.)

This punch is only prepared for parties, and should be mixed as follows

Place 2½ pounds of loaf sugar in the bowl.

5 or 6 bottles of plain soda.

4 lemons, the juice only.

1 qt. of Cognac brandy.

1 small bunch of wintergreen.

4 oranges and 1 pineapple (cut up); and add the slices into the bowl and also strawberries and grapes.

Mix the ingredients well with a ladle and add:

6 bottles of Champagne.

1 bottle brandy.

2 bottles of French claret.

4 bottles of Rhine wine.

1½ gallon of water and mix up well together into the bowl.

This punch must be cold, surrounded with ice, the same as other punches.

After having the entire punch well mixed, take a large fancy goblet, and fill it with the above mixture and dress it with oranges, strawberries and pineapples in season.

Pineapple Punch.

(For a party of 20.)

Take 8 bottles of champagne.

2 pints of Jamaica rum.

2 pints of brandy.

2 gills of Curaçoa.

Juice of 6 lemons.

4 pineapples sliced.

Sweeten to taste with pulverized white sugar.

California Milk Punch.

(For Bottling.)

Juice of 4 lemons.
Rind of 2 lemons.
½ pound of white sugar, dissolved in hot water.
1 pineapple, peeled, sliced and pounded.
6 cloves.
20 coriander seeds.
1 small stick of cinnamon.
1 pint of brandy.
1 pint of Jamaica rum.
1 gill of Batavia arrack.
1 cup of strong green tea.
1 quart of boiling water.
1 quart of hot milk.

Put all the materials in a clean demijohn, the boiling water to be added last.

Cold Ruby Punch.

2 quarts of Batavia arrack.
2 quarts of Port wine.
5 pints of green tea.
2 pounds of loaf sugar.
Juice of 12 lemons.
1 pineapple cut in small pieces.

Sweeten to taste and ice before serving.

Century Club Punch.

1 pint of old Santa Cruz rum.
1 pint of old Jamaica rum.
5 pints of water.

Lincoln Club Punch.

(For a party of twenty-five.)

Take 4 bottles of champagne
1 bottle of pale sherry.
1 bottle of Cognac.
1 bottle of Sauterne.
1 pineapple, sliced and cut in small pieces.
4 lemons, sliced.
Sweeten to taste, mix, cool and serve.

May Wine Punch.

(Use a large punch bowl.)

Take one or two bunches of woodruff, and cut it into small pieces and place it into a large bar glass, and fill up the balance with the best French brandy, cover it up and let it stand for two or three hours, until the essence of the woodruff is thoroughly extracted; cover the bottom of the bowl with loaf sugar, and pour from
 4 to 6 bottles of plain soda over the sugar.
 Cut up 6 oranges in slices.
 ½ pineapple, and sufficient berries and grapes.
 8 bottles of Moselle or Rhine wine.
 1 bottle of Veure Clicquot.
Then put your woodruff and brandy, etc., into the bowl, and then stir well, and you will have 2½ to 3 gallons of excellent May Wine Punch; surround the bowl with ice, serve in a wine glass in such a manner that each customer will get a piece of all of the fruits contained in the punch.

Punch.

Boil a large kettle of strong black coffee, take a large dish and put 4 pounds of sugar into it; then pour 4 bottles of brandy and 2 bottles of Jamaica rum over the sugar, and set it on fire, let the sugar dissolve and drop into the black coffee; stir this well and you will have a good hot punch.

Fishing Punch.

(Use a large bar glass.)

1 table-spoonful of sugar.
1 or 2 dashes of lemon juice.
1 or 2 dashes of lime juice and dissolve in a little water.
And fill glass with fine ice.
1 wine-glass of St. Croix rum.
1 pony glass of brandy.

Stir with a spoon, dress the top with fruit, and serve with a straw.

This drink can be put in bottles for the Fisherman to take along, so that he will loose no time.

Canadian Punch.

(For a party of ten.)

2 quarts of rye whisky.
1 pint of Jamaica rum.
6 lemons, sliced.
1 pineapple, sliced.
4 quarts of water.
Sweeten to taste, and ice before serving.

Bombay Punch.

(Use a large bowl.)

Rub the sugar over the lemons, until it has absorbed all the yellow part of the skins of 6 lemons, then put in the punch bowl:

1 lb. of loaf sugar.
2 bottles of imported seltzer water.
1 pineapple.
6 oranges.
2 lemons.
1 box strawberries.
Mix well with a spoon, and add
4 bottles champagne.
1 bottle of French brandy.
1 bottle of sherry.
1 bottle of Madeira wine.
1 gill of Maraschino.

Stir up well with a ladle, and surround the bowl with ice; and serve in such a manner, that each customer will have some of the fruit.

Punch a la Romaine.

(For a party of twenty.)

2 bottles of rum.
2 bottles of wine.
15 lemons.
3 sweet oranges.
3 pounds of powdered sugar.
15 eggs.

Dissolve the sugar in the juice of the lemons and oranges, adding the thin rind of 1 orange; strain through a sieve into a bowl, and add by degrees the whites of the eggs beaten to a froth. Place the bowl on ice for a while, then stir in briskly the rum and the wine.

English Royal Punch.

(Use a bowl for mixing for a small party.)

1 pint of hot green tea.
½ pint of the best brandy.
½ pint Jamaica rum.
1 wine-glass of Curaçoa (red.)
1 wine-glass of arrac.
Juice of 2 limes.
1 lemon, cut in slices.
¼ lb. of sugar.
Mix this thoroughly with a ladle, and add:
4 eggs, the whites only, and drink this as hot as possible.

If the punch is too strong, add more green tea to taste, and if not hot enough, place the entire mixture over the fire and have it heated, but not boiled, and serve.

Oxford Punch.

1 pint of Cognac brandy.
1 pint of old Jamaica rum.
1 quart of orange shrub.
½ pint of sherry.
1 bottle of Capillaire.
2 quarts of boiling water.
6 glasses of calf's-foot jelly.
6 lemons.
4 sweet oranges.
Sufficient loaf sugar, dissolved in some of the hot water.

Rub the rinds of 3 lemons with sugar. Cut the peel very fine off 2 more lemons and 2 of the oranges. Press out the juice of all the oranges and lemons. Place the whole, with the jelly, in a jug and stir well. Pour on the water, and let it stand for twenty minutes. Strain through a fine sieve into a large bowl; add the Capillaire, spirits, shrub, and wine, stirring well.

Grandeur Punch.

(Use a large bowl.)

1¼ lb. loaf sugar.
6 lemons, cut in slices.
1 gill of Anisette.
1 bottle Kümmel.
6 oranges sliced.
1 bottle of Kirschwasser.
¼ gallon water.
6 bottles of Nordhauser Brantwein.
1 gill of Curaçoa (red.)

Stir well with a ladle, and surround the bowl with ice, and serve in a wine glass.

Empire Punch.

(Use an extra large bowl.)

Rub the peel of 4 fine lemons, and also the peel of two oranges, until it has absorbed all the yellow part of the lemon and orange.

1¼ lb. of lump sugar.
1 pineapple, cut in slices.
12 fine oranges, cut in slices.
1 box of strawberries.
2 bottles Apollinaris water.

Mix the above ingredients well and add:

½ gill of Maraschino.
½ gill of Curaçoa (red.)
½ gill of Benedictine.
½ gill of Jamaica rum.
1 bottle of French brandy.
6 bottles of champagne.
4 bottles of Tokay.
2 bottles of Madeira.
4 bottles of Chateau Margaux.

And mix this well with a ladle, then strain through a sieve into a clean bowl and surround the bowl with ice, and dress the edge with some leaves and fruit, and ornament the punch in a fancy manner with grapes, oranges, pineapple and strawberries.

Saratoga Cocktail.

(Use small bar glass.)

2 dashes Angostura bitters.
3 small lumps of ice.
1 pony of brandy.
1 pony of whisky.
1 pony of Vermouth.

Shake up well, and then strain into into a claret glass, and serve with a slice of lemon.

Cocktail Coffee.

(Use a large bar glass.)

1 tea-spoonful of powdered white sugar.
1 fresh egg.
1 large wine-glass of port wine.
1 pony of best brandy.
2 or 3 lumps of ice.

Break the egg into the glass, put in the sugar, and lastly the port wine, brandy and ice.

Shake up thoroughly, and strain into a medium-sized goblet. Grate a little nutmeg on top before serving.

Morning Cocktail.

(Use medium bar glass.)

3 or 4 dashes of gum syrup.
2 dashes of Curaçoa (red.)
2 dashes of Boker's Bitters.
1 dash of Absinthe.
1 pony of best brandy.
1 pony of whisky.
1 piece of lemon peel, twisted to extract the oil.
3 small lumps of ice.

Stir thoroughly and remove the ice. Fill the glass with seltzer water, and stir with a tea-spoon having a little sugar in it.

Bottle of Cocktail.

1 qt. of good old whisky.
1 pony glass of Curaçoa,
1 wine-glass of gum syrup.
½ pony glass of Angostura bitters.

Mix this well by pouring it from one shaker into another, until it is thoroughly mixed, pour it into a bottle and cork it, and you will have an elegant bottle of Cocktail.

Cocktail Saratoga.

(Use a large bar glass.)

½ glass of fine shaved ice.
3 dashes of pineapple syrup.
2 or 3 dashes of bitters.
3 dashes of Maraschino.
½ glass of fine old brandy.

Mix well with a spoon and place 2 or 3 strawberries in a fancy glass, strain it, twist a piece of lemon peel over it, top it off with a squirt of champagne, and serve.

Claret and Champagne Cup.

(Use a large punch bowl for a party of twenty.)

Claret and Champagne Cup is a Russian drink where for many years it has enjoyed a high reputation amongst the aristocracy. Proportions:

3 bottles claret wine.
½ pint of Curoçoa (red.)
1 pint of sherry.
1 pint of French brandy.
2 wine-glasses of ratafia of raspberries.
3 oranges and one lemon cut in slices.
Some sprigs of green balm, and of borage.
2 bottles of German seltzer water.
3 bottles of soda.

Stir this together, and sweeten with Capillaire pounded sugar, until it ferments; let it stand one hour; strain it and ice it well; it is then fit for use; serve it in small glasses. This quantity for an evening party of twenty persons; for a smaller number reduce the proportions.

Fine Lemonade for Parties.

(Use a punch bowl—1 gallon.)

Take the rind of 8 lemons.
Juice of 12 lemons.
2 lbs. of loaf sugar.
1 gallon of boiling water.

Rub the rinds of the 8 lemons on the sugar until it has absorbed all the oil, and put it with the remainder of the sugar in a jug; add the lemon juice and pour the boiling water over the whole. When the sugar is dissolved, strain the lemonade through a piece of muslin, and when cool, it will be ready for use. To improve the lemonade add the white of 4 eggs beaten up with it.

Jersey Sour.

(Use small bar glass.)

Take 1 large tea-spoonful of powdered sugar dissolved in a little water.
2 or 3 dashes of lemon juice.
1 wine-glass of apple jack.
Fill the glass with ice, shake up, and strain into a claret glass. Ornament with berries in season.

Stone Wall.

(Use a large bar glass.)

¼ table-spoonful of sugar,
3 or 4 lumps of ice.
1 wine-glass of whisky.
1 bottle plain soda.
Stir up well with a spoon, remove the ice and serve.

Whisky Daisy.

(Use small bar glass.)

3 dashes gum syrup.
2 dashes Orgeat syrup.
The juice of half-a small lemon.
1 wine-glass of rye whisky.
Fill glass one-third full of fine ice.
Shake well, strain into a large cocktail glass, and fill up with seltzer water.

Champagne Cup.

(Use a large punch bowl for a party.)

2 wine-glasses of pineapple syrup.
4 to 6 sprigs of green balm.
1 quart of Curaçoa.
1 pint of Chartreuse (green.)
1 quart of fine old Cognac.
1 quart of Tokay.
4 bottles of Apollinaris.
6 oranges and 2 lemons, cut in slices.

Stir up well together, let it stand two hours, strain it into another bowl and add:

½ pineapple cut in slices.
½ box of strawberries.
6 bottles of champagne.

Place the bowl in the ice, and sweeten with a little sugar and let it ferment, stir up well and serve.

Bowl of Egg Nogg for a Party.

For a three gallon bowl mix as follows:

2¼ lbs. of fine powdered sugar.
20 fresh eggs; have the yolks separated; beat as thin as water, and add the yolks of the eggs into the sugar, and dissolve by stirring well together.
2 quarts of good old brandy.
1¼ pints of Jamaica rum.
2 gallons of good rich milk.

Mix the ingredients well, and stir continually while pouring in the milk to prevent it from curdling; then beat the whites of the eggs to a stiff froth and put this on top; then fill a bar glass with a ladle, put some of the egg froth on top, grate a little nutmeg over it and serve.

Champagne Velvet.

(Use a large-sized goblet.)

For this drink a bottle of champagne and a bottle of port must be used.

Fill the glass ½ full with porter, the balance with champagne.

Stir up with a spoon slowly, and you have what is call. Champagne Velvet.

Boston Egg Nogg.

(Use a large bar glass.)

Yolk of an egg.
¾ table-spoonful of powdered sugar.
Add a little nutmeg and cinnamon, and beat to a cream.
½ pony glass of brandy.
1 wine-glassful of ice.
¼ pony glass of Jamaica rum.
1 wine-glassful of Madeira wine.

Fill the glass with milk, shake well, strain into a large bar glass, grate a little nutmeg on top and serve.

Apple Toddy.

(Use medium bar glass, hot.)

1 large tea-spoonful of fine white sugar dissolved in a little boiling hot water.
1 wine-glass of apple jack.
¼ of a baked apple.

Fill the glass two-thirds full of boiling water, stir up, and grate a little nutmeg on top. Serve with a spoon.

Pineapple Julep.

(For a party of five.)

The juice of two oranges.
1 gill of raspberry syrup.
1 gill of Maraschino.
1 gill of Old Tom gin.
1 quart bottle Sparkling Moselle.
1 ripe pineapple, peeled and sliced small and cut up.

Put all the materials in a glass bowl; ice, and serve i cocktail glasses, ornamented with berries in season.

Whisky and Cider.

(Use a whisky glass.)

Hand the bottle of whisky to the customer to help himself, fill up the glass with good apple cider, stir well with a spoon, and serve, and you will have a very nice drink.

Santa Cruz Rum Daisy.

(Use small bar glass.)

3 or 4 dashes of rum syrup.
2 or 3 dashes of Curaçoa.
The juice of half a lemon.
1 wine-glass of Santa Cruz rum.
Fill glass one-third full of shaved ice.

Shake thoroughly, strain into a large cocktail glass, and fill up with seltzer water.

Santa Cruz Fix.

(Use small bar glass.)

1 large tea-spoonful of powdered sugar, dissolved in a little water.
2 dashes of Curaçoa.
The juice of half a lemon.
A wine-glass of Santa Cruz rum.

Fill up the glass two thirds full of shaved ice, stir well and ornament the top with a slice of orange and a piece of pineapple.

Whisky Daisy.

(Use a large bar glass.)

½ table-spoonful of sugar.
3 or 4 dashes of lemon juice.
1 dash of lime juice.
1 pony glass of brandy, seltzer, dissolve with the lemon and lime juice.
¾ of the glass filled with fine ice.
1 wine-glass of good whisky.
Fill the glass with shaved ice.
½ pony glass Chartreuse, stir well, then take a fancy glass have it dressed with fruit, strain and serve.

Milk and Seltzer.

(Use a medium-sized bar glass.)

In serving this drink, which is strictly temperance, to half fill the glass with seltzer, and the rest with milk; if it is don otherwise you will have nothing but foam in your glass, which would cause delay.

Cider Egg Nogg.

(Use a large bar glass.)

1 fresh egg.
¼ table-spoonful of sugar.
3 or 4 small lumps of ice.
Fill the glass with cider.
Shake well and strain, grate a little nutmeg on top.

This drink is a very pleasant one, and is popular throughout the southern part of the country and it is not intoxicating. Use the very best quality of cider, as by using poor cider it is impossible to make this drink palatable.

Brace Up Saratoga.

(Use large bar glass.)

1 table-spoonful of fine white sugar.
2 or 3 dashes of Boker's bitters.
3 or 4 dashes of lime juice.
2 dashes of Absinthe.
1 fresh egg.
1 wine-glass of brandy.
2 small lumps of ice.

Shake thoroughly, strain into another glass, and fill with seltzer water.

Couperee.

(Use large soda glass.)

Take 1½ pony-glass of brandy.
1 pony-glass Curaçoa (red.)
Fill the glass one-third full of ice cream.

Mix thoroughly, and fill the glass nearly full with plain soda. Grate a little nutmeg on top, and serve.

Crimean Cup a La Marmora.

(Use a bowl for mixing.)

1 pint of Orgeat syrup.
½ pint of Cognac.
¼ pint of Maraschino.
¼ pint Jamaica rum.
1 bottle champagne.
1 bottle of soda.
6 ounces of sugar.
2 lemons and 2 oranges, cut in slices.
And a few slices of pineapple.

Stir up well with ladle, then place it into your dish filled with ice, and serve.

Santa Cruz Sour.

(Use small bar glass.)

1 large tea-spoonful of white sugar dissolved in a little Apollinaris water.
3 dashes of lemon juice.
1 wine-glass of Santa Cruz rum.

Fill the glass full of shaved ice, shake up and strain into a claret wine glass, ornament with orange and berries in season.

How to Serve a Pony Glass of Brandy.

(Use a pony glass.)

The latest style of serving a pony of brandy, is to place the pony at the edge of the counter, then take a whisky tumbler upside down in the left hand, and place it over the pony glass of brandy, then reverse the glass, as well as the pony glass containing the brandy, so as to have the stem of the pony glass on top, and the brandy at the bottom of the whisky glass, in order to be convenient for the customer.

Beef Tea.

(Use a hot water glass.)

¼ tea-spoonful of the best beef extract.
Fill the glass with hot water.
Stir up well with a spoon, place pepper, salt and celery salt handy, and if the customer should require it, put in a small pony of sherry wine or brandy.

Tom Collins.

(Use an extra large bar glass.)

½ table-spoonful of sugar.
3 or 4 dashes of lime juice.
3 or 4 pieces of broken ice.
1 wine-glass of Old Tom gin.
1 bottle of plain soda.
Mix well with a spoon, strain and serve.
Attention must be paid not to let the foam of the soda spread over the glass; this drink must be drank as soon as mixed.

Brace Up.

(Use a large bar glass.)

1 table-spoonful of white sugar.
2 or 3 dashes of bitters.
2 or 3 dashes of lemon juice
1 dash of lime juice.
2 dashes of Anisette
1 fresh egg.
¾ glass of brandy.
½ glass of shaved ice.
Shake this up thoroughly in a shaker, strain it into a large glass, and fill with vichy or Apollinaris water and serve.

Brandy Shrub.

(Use bowl—to make 8 quarts.)

6 lbs. of loaf sugar, dissolve well with a bottle of plain soda.

5 quarts of old brandy.
3 quarts of sherry.
12 lemons.

Peel the rind of 5 lemons; add the juice of the other 7 lemons and mix with brandy into the bowl, cover it close for 5 days, then add the sherry and sugar, strain through a bag, and bottle.

Currant Shrub.

(Use a bowl for mixing ; general rule for preparing.)

1 quart of currant juice.
1¼ lbs. of loaf sugar.

Boil it gently 8 or 10 minutes, skimming it well; take it off, and when lukewarm, add ¼ gill of brandy to every pint of shrub. Bottle tight.

Mix a little shrub with ice water and you will have a delicious drink. Shrub may be made of cherry or raspberry juice by this method, but the quantity of sugar must be reduced.

Soda Negus.

(Use a small punch bowl; about 1 quart.)

1 pint of Port wine.
12 lumps of loaf sugar.
8 cloves.

Grated nutmeg sufficient to fill a small tea-spoon; put the above ingredients into a thoroughly clean saucepan, warm and stir them well, but do not suffer it to boil; upon the warm wine empty a bottle of plain soda. This makes a delicious and refreshing drink.

Claret Cup for a Party.

(Use a bowl for mixing.)

10 to 12 pieces of lump sugar.
1 bottle of Apollinaris.
2 lemons, 2 oranges and ¼ pineapple, cut in slices.
2 wine-glasses of Maraschino.

Mix well with a ladle, place this into your vessel or tin dish filled with ice, when the party is ready to call for it, add:

4 bottles fine claret.
1 bottle of champagne, or any other sparkling wine.

Mix thoroughly and place sufficient berries on top and serve it, and you will have an elegant Claret Cup.

Bottled Velvet.

(Use a punch bowl.)

1 quart bottle of Moselle.
½ pint of sherry wine.
2 table-spoonfuls of sugar.
1 lemon.
1 sprig of verbena.

Peel the lemon very thin, using only sufficient of the peel to produce the desired flavor; add the other ingredients strain and ice.

Balaklavo Nectar.

(For a party of fifteen.)

Thinly peel the rind of ½ lemon, shred it fine, and put it in a punch bowl, add 4 table-spoonfuls of crushed sugar and the juice of one lemon.

1 gill of Maraschino.
2 bottles of soda.
2 bottles of claret wine.
2 bottles of champagne.

Stir well together and dress the top with fruit in season.

Punch a La Fork.

(For bottling.)

2 lbs. of loaf sugar.
3 dozen lemons.
1 pint of Cognac.
1 pint Jamacia rum.

The lemons should have smooth rinds; peel the yellow rinds off quite thin with a sharp knife, place them in an earthen vessel; add the sugar, and stir thoroughly for nearly half an hour to extract the essential oil. Pour on boiling water, and stir until the sugar is completely dissolved.

Cut and squeeze the lemon, straining the juice from the pits. Place the pits in a jug and pour boiling water upon them to obtain the mucilage from them. Pour ½ of the lemon juice into the syrup, strain the water from the pits, and add it also to the syrup, taking care that the syrup is not too watery.

Next, add more sugar or lemon juice, to make the mixture according to the taste.

Lastly, add and stir in the above amount of spirits into every 3 quarts of lemonade, and bottle. Keep in a cool place.

Fedora.

(Use a large bar glass.)

1 pony of the best brandy.
1 pony of Curaçoa.
½ pony of Jamaica rum.
½ pony of Bourbon.
1 table-spoonful of sugar, dissolved in a little water.
1 slice of lemon.

Fill the tumbler with fine ice; shake well and ornament with berries or small pieces of orange, serve with a straw.

Bishop a La Prusse.

1 bottle of Port wine.
¼ lb. of pounded loaf sugar.
5 good-sized bitter oranges.

Roast the oranges until they are of a pale brown color; lay them in a tureen, and cover them with the sugar, adding 3 glasses of the Port wine; cover the tureen and let it stand until the next day. When required for use, place the tureen in a pan of boiling water, press the oranges with a spoon, and run the juice through a sieve. Boil the remainder of the Port wine; add the strained juice, and serve warm in glasses.

Curacoa.

6 ounces of very thin orange peel.
1 pint of whisky.
1 pint of clarified syrup.
1 drachm powdered alum.
1 drachm Carbonate of potash.

Place the orange peel in a bottle, which will hold a quart with the whisky; cork tightly and let the contents remain for 12 days, shaking the bottle frequently. Then strain out the peel, add the syrup; shake well, and let it stand for 3 days. Take out a tea-cupful into a mortar, and beat up with the alum and potash; when well mixed, pour it back into the bottle, and let it remain for a week. The Curaçoa will then be perfectly clear.

Frapped Cafe Royal.

It consists of three-fourths of black coffee and one-fourth brandy, frappéd in a cooler, and drank while the mixture is yet in a semi-frozen state. It is very potent.

Manhattan Club Oyster Cocktail.

Take the piece of ½ a lemon, strain into a large goblet.
1 or 2 dashes Tabaso sauce.
1 tea-spoonful of pepper sauce.
A trace of vinegar.
A pint of salt.
A little red pepper.
A slightly larger quantity of white pepper.

This entire array forms but the seasoning for the liquor of half a dozen freshly opened, succulent Blue Point oysters, which is next added to the contents of the glass, and completes the cocktail.

INVALIDS' DRINKS.

Rice Water.

Take best Carolina or Patna rice, should be washed with cold water, then boiled in a good measure of water for ten minutes, the water strained off, and more added ; and so on till the goodness is boiled out of the rice. The water is ready to drink when cold. Cream may be added if there be not high fever; a pinch of salt also, if desired, or flavoring as for barley water.

White Wine Whey.

Put two pints of new milk in a saucepan, and stir it over a clear fire till it is nearly boiling ; then add a quarter of a pint of sherry, and simmer for a quarter of an hour, skimming off the curd as it rises. Then add a table-spoonful more sherry, and skim again for a few minutes, till the whey is clear; sweeten with loaf sugar, if required.

Lime Water.

Pour over a piece of fresh unslacked lime, about an inch square, two quarts of hot water. When it has slacked (in a few minutes) stir it thoroughly. Let it remain over night. Bottle carefully all the liquid that can be poured off in perfectly clear state.

As water will only hold a certain amount of lime in solution, the addition of more lime would make the water of no great strength.

Lime water (an alkali) is generally added to milk for the purpose of neutralizing the effects of an acid stomach.

About a tea-spoonful to a table-spoonful of lime water to a half pint of milk is usually prescribed.

Barley Water.

Add to a pint of boiling water half a table-spoonful (half an ounce) of barley, rubbed smooth, with two table-spoonfuls of cold water; add also a pinch of salt and a table-spoonful of sugar. Let it boil five minutes. It is to be drank cold. The simple barley water has not an unpleasant taste, and is often prepared without additional flavor. Yet zest *i. e.*, the thin yellow cuts of the rind of a lemon, or lump sugar rubbed over to extract the oil, can be added as flavoring, or a lemonade may be made of barley water.

Barley water may be used temporarily instead of milk.

Oatmeal Drink.

Rub two table-spoonfuls (two ounces) of oatmeal smooth by gradually stirring in a tea-cupful of cold water; add a pinch of salt. Stir this into a quart of boiling water and let it boil half an hour. Strain it through a fine sieve.

Tamarind Water.

Stir into a glassful of water a table-spoonful of preserved tamarinds.

Cinnamon Water.

Add five or six sticks (half an ounce) of cinnamon to a pint of boiling water, and boil fifteen minutes.

To be administered by the table-spoonful.

Given for hemorrhages.

Toast Water.

Toast thoroughly thin slices of graham bread, and break them into a bowl. Pour over enough boiling water to cover it when cold; strain off the water and sweeten it slightly. Serve it always freshly made.

Currant Jelly Water.

(FOR FEVER PATIENTS.)

A tea-spoonful of currant jelly, dissolve in a goblet of water, and sweeten to taste, affords a refreshing drink for invalids.

Flaxseed Tea.

Add half a cupful of flaxseed to four cupfuls, or a quart, of boiling water. Let it boil half an hour. Let it stand fifteen or twenty minutes near the fire, after it has boiled. Of course the longer it stands the thicker it becomes. Strain, sweeten to taste, and add a little lemon-juice, or not, as preferred.

This is a useful demulcent drink for coughs, etc.

Flaxseed and Licorice Tea.

Pour one pint of boiling water over one ounce of flaxseed, not bruised, and two drachms of licorice-root bruised, and place the covered vessel near the fire for four hours. Strain it through a sieve.

Wine, Lemon, or Vinegar Whey.

When a pint of milk is brought just to boil, pour in a gill of sherry wine. Let it again come to a boil. When the whey separates, strain and sweeten to taste, using perhaps a tea-spoonful of sugar.

Or the whey can be made in the same manner with lemon-juice (free from seeds), using the juice of half a lemon instead of wine, a table-spoonful being quite enough for a pint of milk.

In an alimentary point of view, whey is almost of no value. It is advantageous as a drink in febrile diseases, and is a good means of administering wine in small quantities.

It may be drank either cold or warm.

It possesses sudorific and diuretic properties.

Simple Beverages from Fruits.

Currant jelly water (or any acid jelly—cranberry, plum, etc.)

If the jelly is soft, a tea-spoonful is dissolved in a goblet of fresh cold water, and sweetened to taste.

If the jelly is hard, it will have to be added to boiling water to become dissolved. To be drank cold.

The fresh fruits are, of course, to be preferred.

There is nothing more refreshing than currant water made from fresh currants.

This can be prepared by allowing a pint of water to a pint of currants (freed from stems) and a table-spoonful of sugar.

Heat these slowly in a porcelain or granitized iron kettle until it boils, then let it simmer for five minutes. Strain it through a cloth, let cool, and sweeten again to taste. It can be diluted with water.

If strawberries, raspberries, black raspberries, or blackberries are used, prepare them in the same manner, excepting that for each quart of berries a pint of water with a table-spoonful of sugar should be used.

Grape Juice.

Allow one pint of water to three pints of fruit (picked from stems). Let it simmer slowly for five minutes, then strain it through flannel or cheese cloth. It is drank cold without sweetening. Add a little sugar if not sweet enough.

Apple Water.

(The same for any of the fruits, viz.: pears, peaches, plums, French prunes, figs, raisins, rhubarb, etc.)

Boil a large, juicy apple, (pared, cored and cut into pieces) in a pint of water in a close-covered saucepan, until the apple is stewed into a pulp. Strain the liquor, pressing all the juice from the pulp. Sweeten to taste. Sometimes these fruit-waters are made with rice or barley water. To be drank cold.

TEMPERANCE DRINKS.

Lemonade.

(Fine for parties.)

Rind of 2 lemons.
Juice of 3 large lemons.
¼ lb. of loaf sugar.
1 qt. boiling water.

Rub some of the sugar in lumps on two of the lemons until they have imbibed all the oil from them, and put it with the remainder of the sugar into a jug; add the lemon juice (but no pips), and pour over the whole a quart of boiling water. When the sugar is dissolved strain the lemonade through a piece of muslin, and, when cool, it will be ready for use.

The lemonade will be much improved by having the white of an egg beaten up with it; a little sherry mixed with it also makes this beverage much nicer.

Lemonade.

(Use large bar glass.)

Juice of ½ lemon.
1½ tablespoonful of sugar.
2 or 3 pieces of orange.
1 tablespoonful of raspberry or strawberry syrup.

DRAUGHT LEMONADE.

Fill the tumbler half full with shaved ice, the balance with water; dash with port wine, and ornament with fruits in season.

Ginger Lemonade.

Boil ten pounds and a half of lump sugar for twenty minutes in ten gallons of water; clear it with the whites of six eggs. Bruise half a pound of common ginger, boil with the liquor, and then pour it upon ten lemons pared. When quite cold put it in a cask, with two tablespoonfuls of yeast, the lemons sliced, and half an ounce of isinglass. Bung up the cask the next day; it will be ready in two weeks.

Lemonade Powders.

1 lb. finely-powdered loaf sugar.
1 oz. tartaric or citric acid.
20 drops essence of lemon.
Mix, and keep very dry.

Two or three teaspoonfuls of this stirred briskly in a tumbler of water will make a very pleasant glass of lemonade. If effervescent lemonade be desired, ¼ oz. of carbonate of soda must be added to the above.

Draught Lemonade, or Lemon Sherbet.

5 lemons, sliced.
4 oz. lump sugar.
1 qt. boiling water.
Very fine.

Draught Lemonade, or Lemon Sherbet.

(A cheaper method.)

1½ oz. cream of tartar.
1½ oz. tartaric or citric acid.
Juice and peel of three lemons.
2 lb. or more loaf sugar.
The sweetening must be regulated according to taste.

Imperial Drink for Families.

3 oz. cream of tartar.
Juice and peel of 3 or 4 lemons.
2 lb. coarse sugar.
Put these into a gallon pitcher and pour on boiling water. When cool, it will be fit for use.

Soda Nectar.

Juice of 1 lemon.
½ tumblerful of water.
Powdered white sugar to taste.
½ small teaspoonful carbonate of soda.

Strain the juice of the lemon, and add it to the water, with sufficient white sugar to sweeten the whole nicely. When well mixed put in the soda, stir well, and drink while the mixture is in an effervescing state.

Sherbet.

10 oz. carbonate of soda.
8 oz. tartaric acid.
3 lbs. loaf sugar, finely powdered.
4 dr. essence of lemon.
Let the powders be very dry. Mix them intimately,

and keep them for use in a wide-mouthed bottle closely corked.

Put two good-sized teaspoonfuls into a tumbler; pour in half a pint of cold water, stir briskly, and drink off.

Nectar.

1 dr. citric acid.
1 sc. bicarbonate of potash.
1 oz. white sugar, powdered.

Fill a soda-water bottle nearly full of water, drop in the potash and sugar, and lastly the citric acid. Cork the bottle up immediately and shake. As soon as the crystals are dissolved the nectar is fit for use. It may be colored with a small portion of cochineal.

Raspberry, Strawberry, Currant, or Orange Effervescing Draughts.

Take one quart of the juice of either of the above fruits, filter it, and boil it into a syrup, with one pound of powdered loaf sugar. To this add one ounce and a half of tartaric acid. When cold put it into a bottle and keep it well corked. When required, fill a half-pint tumbler three-parts full of water, and add two tablespoonfuls of the syrup. Then stir in briskly a small teaspoonful of carbonate of soda. The color may be improved by adding a small portion of cochineal to the syrup at the time of boiling.

Orangeade.

This agreeable beverage is made the same way as lemonade, substituting oranges for lemons.

CORDIALS.

Aniseed.

¼ oz. oil of aniseed.
5 pints spirit of wine (60 O. P.).
11 pints cordial syrup.
First dissolve the oil in the spirit by shaking both well together in the jar, and then add the syrup, again agitating briskly. Should the mixture be at all cloudy, fine with alum and salts of tartar.

Carraway.

¼ oz. English oil of carraway.
3½ pints of spirit of wine (60 O. P.).
13 pints cordial spirit.
Dissolve the oil in the spirit as above, add the syrup, and if necessary fine with alum and tartar.

Cloves.

¼ oz. English oil of cloves.
5 pints rectified spirit (60 O. P.).
Coloring, a sufficiency.
11 pints cordial syrup.
Dissolve the oil in the spirit as before, add the syrup, shake all together, and if not bright in a few hours, fine with alum and tartar.

Cinnamon.

¼ oz. oil of cinnamon.
5 pints rectified spirit (60 O. P.).
10 pints cordial syrup.
4 pints boiling water.
Color with burned sugar.

The oil and coloring matter should be well shaken with a small quantity of spirit, then added to the remainder and the whole agitated briskly. Add the boiling water to the syrup, and having mixed them let them be added to the jar containing the spirit. If necessary, fine down with alum, etc., as with the others. In making the above a considerable saving may be effected by using oil of cassia ; the true cinnamon flavor is, of course, wanting, but is so well represented by that of oil of cassia that none but the most experienced can detect the difference.

Cordial Syrup.

35 lbs. refined lump sugar.
3 gallons boiling water.

Dissolve the sugar in the water and stir in through flannel.

Capillaire.

20 lbs. best lump sugar.
10 pts. water.
1 drachm acetic acid, strong.

Boil the sugar in the water till it is all dissolved ; add the acetic acid, and allow it to remain ten or fifteen minutes on the fire : remove and allow it to cool ; then decant ; clear into a bottle or jar.

Ginger Brandy.

This may be made by following the same directions as given for ginger gin, or the following will be found more economical, though taking a longer time to prepare. Steep half a pound of well bruised Jamaica ginger in one gallon of strong brandy for fourteen days, shaking it up repeatedly. Let this be strained through muslin. Throw the ginger from the muslin into a gallon of boiling water and allow it to simmer over a low fire for twenty minutes and strain. To this add ten pounds of refined sugar.

Peppermint.

1 drachm oil of peppermint.
3 pints rectified spirit (60 O. P.).
13 pints cordial syrup.
Proceed as in the foregoing.

Ginger.

Bruise half a pound of the best new Jamaica ginger in an iron mortar, and put it into a bottle containing one pint of spirit of wine (60 O. P.), and one pint of water, allow it to macerate for ten or twelve days, shaking it up well each morning. After the twelfth day transfer it to a funnel containing a paper filter; when all the liquid has run through pass two pints of sherry over it, and lastly, one pint of boiling water. This will yield rather better than half a gallon of liquid. When all are mixed, dissolve in this one ounce of burned sugar, and having added twelve pints of syrup, shake the whole well up, and fine with alum, etc.

Ginger Gin.

Take of best Jamaica ginger, bruised small, half a pound ; boil it in one gallon of water, and strain through fine muslin. In this dissolve ten pounds of refined sugar by means of a gentle heat. Over the bruised ginger which remains in the muslin strainer pass one gallon unmixed gin (O. P.), mix this and the syrup of ginger together, add finings, and set aside to clear.

Usquebaugh.

1 drachm oil of aniseed.
1 drachm oil of cloves.
1 drachm essential oil of nutmegs.
20 drops oil of cinnamon.
30 drops oil of juniper.

Mix all the oils together, shaking well occasionally for a day or so ; then dissolve them in rectified spirit (60 O. P.), one pint; colored with burned sugar, one ounce ; and add of each, syrup and boiling water, twelve pints. Mix all together thoroughly and fine with alum, etc.

Rum Shrub.

½ gallon bitter orange juice.
8 lbs. refined sugar.
1½ gallon rum, reduced to 40 U. P.

Dissolve the sugar in the juice by aid of a gentle heat, mix this and the rum together, shake up well and set aside to clear. If not bright in a fortnight fine down with isinglass.

Raspberry.

8 oz. essence of raspberry.
2½ pints spirit of wine (53 O. P.).
13 pints cordial syrup.
2 oz. tincture of cudbear, strong.

Let all these be shaken well up together in a jar, using no finings, for if the materials are genuine, the cordial will be bright and ready for use the day it is mixed.

Strawberry.

7 oz. essence of strawberry.
4 pts. rectified spirit 60 O. P.).
3 oz. tincture of cudbear.
14 pts. cordial syrup.

Proceed as with raspberry.

Lemon.

3 drops essential oil of lemon.
3 pts. lemon juice.
6 oz. lemon peel, fresh.
6 lbs. refined sugar.
2 pts. rectified spirit.

Add the oil to the juice, and in it boil the peel, which should be cut very small, and strain; add to the strained liquor the sugar; dissolve by aid of gentle heat, and when cool, mix in the spirit by brisk agitation.

Curacoa Cordial.

1 lb. orange peel.
¼ lb. ground cinnamon.
16 oranges.
6 galls. white syrup.
Boil 5 minutes.

Add 3 galls. pure spirits, 95 per cent. above; filter through Canton flannel and bottle.

Maraschino Cordial.

3½ galls. 95 per cent. spirits.
7 " white syrup.
1 " peach juice.

Filter through Canton flannel; bottle for use.

Lemon Extract.

1 oz. oil of lemon.
48 " citric acid (tincture.)
6 galls. gum syrup.

Put in enough water to make 24 gallons.
Before mixing, cut the oil in a pint of alcohol.
Filter carefully through charcoal.

Banana Syrup.

1 gall. white syrup.
1 oz. essence of banana.
A few drops lemon extract.

Blackberry Extract.

Mash nice blackberries; strain through flannel; to 1 pint of juice add

1 lb. crushed sugar.
½ oz. ground cinnamon.
¼ " mace.

2 table-spoons powdered sugar.
Boil the whole 15 minutes.
Strain ; and if you wish, add ¼ gill of brandy.

Ginger Syrup, No. 1.

1 gallon white syrup.
12 ounces tincture of ginger.
Strain if cloudy.

Ginger Syrup, No. 2.

Put 2 ounces Jamaica ginger into a quart of boiling water, let it remain 24 hours, closely covered, strain, and add 3 pounds crushed sugar; boil to a syrup.

Lemon Syrup.

5 gallons gum syrup.
8 ounces tartaric acid (tincture.)
1 ounce oil of lemon, cut in 1 pint of alcohol.

Orgeat Syrup.

3 ounces powdered sugar.
3 ounces sweet almonds.
½ ounce bitter almonds.
¼ pound powdered gum arabic.
Pound altogether, adding a little water, until it meas. ures 1 quart. Strain, and add 2 gallons syr

CONCENTRATED FRUIT SYRUPS.

The strength of all the following syrups has been calculated solely with a view to the convenience of hotel keepers, etc. We advise each party to prepare them for themselves; and this can be done with little or no trouble, by making two or three gallons of the simple syrup as a stock, from which a pint or two can be taken at any time, and flavored with any of the fruit essences as required. In summer, one ounce added to a bottle of aerated water or soda water, will produce a glass of orangeade, lemonade, nectar, or other such beverage as may be required, thus obviating the necessity of keeping a stock of each of these in bottle. In winter they may be used instead of sugar for sweetening hot drinks, such as gin, rum, etc., to which they impart the agreeable flavor of fruit whose name they bear. They are also used as a base for the various acidulated summer beverages.

Simple Syrup.

7 lbs. refined sugar.
3 pts. distilled water.
Dissolve the sugar in the water over a gentle fire.

Clove Syrup.

30 drops of quintessence of cloves.
1 lb. simple syrup.
Mix by shaking well up together in a bottle.

Orange Syrup.

2 oz. tincture of orange-peel.
1 lb. simple syrup.
Mix.

Syrup of Nectar.

30 drops essence of nectar.
1 lb. simple syrup.
Mix.

The proportion of 30 parts of sugar to 16 parts of water also makes an excellent syrup.

It is worth adding that it will be found best to employ only the best refined sugar, and filtered water, soft as possible. By so doing it often saves the trouble of clarification, which invariably becomes necessary when inferior ingredients are used.

The best plan is to pour the water cold over the sugar and let it slowly melt; and, when saturated, boil it up to the boil by a gentle heat, and then keep simmering to the point desired.

Pineapple Syrup.

Add 1 ounce essence of pineapple to 1 gallon white syrup and half ounce tartaric acid.

Raspberry Syrup

1 gallon white syrup.
¼ ounce essence of raspberry.
¼ ounce tincture tartaric acid.

Sarsaparilla Syrup.

10 drops oil of anise.
20 drops oil of wintergreen.
20 drops oil of sassafras.
6 ounces of caramel.
Cut the oils in 4 ounces alcohol.

Strawberry Syrup.

1 gallon white syrup.
1 ounce essence strawberry.
1 ounce tartaric acid.
Color with tincture solferino.

Vanilla Syrup.

1 gallon white syrup.
½ ounce extract vanilla.

Wild Cherry Syrup.

4 ounces wild cherry bark, steeped in a pint of cold water 36 hours; press out, and add half pound sugar. Strain.

LIQUEURS.

Anisette.

10 oz. powdered aniseed.
1 oz. powdered cummin seed.
1 oz. powdered orris root.
3 oz. lemon peel.
2 gallons spirit (30 U. P.).
3 pts. capillaire.

Macerate the powders and the peel in the spirit for about a month, then filter and add the capillaire.

Aqua Bianca.

¼ oz. essence of lemon.
¼ oz. essence of citron.
¼ oz. essence of amber.
¼ oz. essence of peppermint.
¼ oz. essence of bergamot.
½ oz. essence of rose.
2 gallons proof spirit.
5 pints capillaire.

Mix all together; shake frequently, and in one month filter through flannel.

Cordiale De Caladon.

½ lb. lemon peel, cut small.
½ oz. fennel seed, in coarse powder.
¼ oz. cardamoms.
1 drachm aniseed.
1 drachm cloves.
2 gallons proof spirit.
4 pints capillaire.

Macerate the peel and the powders in the spirit for fourteen days, then press and filter, and add the capillaire.

Citron.

12 oz. lemon peel.
1 oz. essence of saffron.
2 gallons proof spirit.
½ gallon capillaire.

Macerate the peel in the spirit for fourteen days, then add the essence of saffron and capillaire.

Citrionette.

2¼ gallons proof spirit.
¼ gallon orange flower water.
½ gallon syrup.
10 oz. lemon peel.
1½ oz. essence of saffron.
¼ oz. essence of amber.
¼ oz. essence of orange.
1 drachm essence of bergamot.

Mix altogether, and in one month press and filter. This is greatly improved by age.

Eau D'Absinthe.

33 oz. wormwood.
24 oz. refined sugar.
4 oz. juniper berries.
¼ oz. angelica root.
1 oz. cinnamon bark.
4 oz. orange flower water.
2½ gallons spirit of wine (11 U. P.).

Bruise the sugar, berries, wormwood, etc., in an iron mortar or other convenient utensil and place them in a wide mouthed jar, then add the orange water and spirit. Stir them well up every day for a month, then press and filter.

Eau D'Amis.

4 oz. figs.
4 oz. raisins.
4 oz. dates.
1 oz. essence of saffron.
6 drops essence of bergamot.
10 drops essence of citron.
1 1-2 gallons proof spirit.
10 lbs. brown sugar.
6 pints distilled water.

Beat up the figs, dates, etc., with a part of the sugar until they form a paste; place this in a wide-mouthed jar, and having previously mixed together the liquids, add a quart at a time, stirring well between each addition; lastly, add the balance of the sugar, and in one month press and filter.

Eau de Cordiale.

20 oz. lemon peel.
4 oz. cinnamon bark, bruised.
2 oz. balm, the fresh herb.
2 oz. powdered coriander seed.
2 oz. powdered aniseed.
1 oz. powdered mace.
1 oz. powdered nutmeg.
2½ gallons rectified spirit (60 O. P.).
2 gallons distilled water.
1 gallon capillaire.

Macerate the solids for ten days in the spirits, and decant as much liquor as can be got off clear. To the mace add the water and capillaire; stir well up and set aside for fourteen days; then press, filter and add the liquor first withdrawn. Another method, and we think a better one, is to mix all the ingredients together, and stir them well up every other morning for about a month, and then to press and filter.

Curacao.

6 oz. orange peel, cut small.
1 drachm cinnamon.
1-2 drachm mace, bruised.
1 drachm saffron.
1 ¼ gallons spirit of wine (14 U. P.).
2 pints capillaire.

Macerate all together; in about twenty-one days draw off the liquor through a strainer, and press the residue so as to recover any of the liquor it may have retained; mix both liquors, and filter through flannel.

BITTERS.

Orange Bitters.

1¼ lb. freshly dried orange peel.
1½ oz. coriander seeds.
1¼ drachm carraway seeds.
1½ drachm cardamom seeds.
6 pts. rectified spirits (60 O. P.).
3 oz. burned sugar.
7 pts. syrup.
Water, sufficient to make up two gallons.

Steep the seeds and peel in the spirit for fourteen or twenty days, when it must be drained off and replaced by water ; which after two days drain off and replace by a second quantity of water. Let the three tinctures thus obtained be mixed together, and first the coloring and then the syrup be added. This, if allowed to remain a short time undisturbed, will become bright ; or if wanted for immediate use, may be filtered through fine linen.

Wormwood Bitters.

2 drops oil of lemon.
2 drops oil of carraway.
2 drops of oil absinthe.

2 oz. extract of licorice.
¼ oz. extract of chamomile.
3 pints rectified spirit (60 O. P.).
3 pints syrup.
Water, enough to make two gallons.

Dissolve the oils in the spirit, and the extracts in water, add both together at once, shake violently for some minutes ; next add the syrup and the remainder of the water, and again shake well up. Let it stand aside some days, the longer the better, then filter through paper.

Angostura Bitters.

4 oz. Angustura bark.
1 oz. chamomile flowers.
¼ oz. cardamom seeds.
¼ oz. cinnamon bark.
1 oz. orange peel.
1 lb. raisins.
2½ gallons proof spirit.

Macerate for a month, then press and filter.

Wine Bitters.

1 thin peel of lemon.
1 thin peel of bitter orange.
3 oz. good sherry.
2 oz. water.
Infuse.

Brandy Bitters.

4 lbs. gentian root.
2 lbs. cardamom seeds.
1 lb. cinnamon bark.
¼ lb. cochineal.
2 lbs. chireta.

Bruise all these together to the size of barley corns; then add two gallons of brandy. Macerate for about a month, then press out all the liquid; to the residue add one gallon more brandy (some use plain spirit), and after having allowed it to stand one day, press as before; add the two liquids and filter, when it will be ready for use.

Dutch Bitters.

2 oz. wormwood.
1 oz. chamomile flowers.
1 oz. gentian root.
2 oz. orange peel.
⅛ oz. powdered cloves.
¼ oz. carraway seeds.
½ gallon capillaire.
2 gallons proof spirit.

Macerate for a month, then press and filter.

Bitters.

1 lb. raisins.
3 oz. bruised cinnamon.
1 oz. Virginia snake root.
Juice of 1 orange and 1 lemon.
20 cloves.

Digest in rum for two months.

Essence of Bitters.

¼ lb. orange peel, dried.
¼ lb. orange apples.
½ lb. gentian root.
¼ lb. lemon peel, ground to powder.

Macerate for ten days. Add one gallon of pure spirit. Strain with pressure. Add one quart of soft water.

"Pick-Me-Up" Bitters.

1 oz. Angostura bark.
1 oz. orange peel.
1 oz. lemon peel.
½ oz. chireta.
½ oz. chamomile flowers.
¼ oz. cardamom seeds.
¼ oz. cinnamon bark.
¼ oz. carraway seeds.
4 lbs. raisins.
1¼ gallons spirits (11 U. P.).

Macerate for a month, then press and filter.

Quinine Bitters.

160 grains sulphate of quinine.
1 lb. orange peel, cut small.
2 gallons cape wine.
1 pt. proof spirit.

Dissolve the quinine in the spirit by aid of a gentle heat, and pour it over the orange peel. After it has been allowed to remain undisturbed in a close vessel for two days add the wine, and stir up well every day for a fortnight, then press and filter.

MINERAL WATERS.

In order to make mineral water properly, it is absolutely necessary to possess a powerful aerating and bottling machine, and the water must be, with the carbonic acid gas and chemicals, of the purest quality ; the corks used must also be excellent and especially prepared.

Aerated Chalybeate Water

Contains pro-sulphate of iron, and bicarbonate of potassa. It is a very easy and excellent mode of introducing iron into the blood, and is much recommended on that account, possessing equal tonic properties to that of the natural springs.

Carbonated Lime Water

Is an aerated solution of bicarbonate of lime ; the best is made from calcined Carara marble, each bottle containing eight or ten grains of carbonate of lime ; it is administered to strengthen the bony structure.

Lithia Water

Is a solution of the freshly precipitated carbonate of lithia ; this water is becoming popular, being useful in calculous complaints.

Magnesia Water

Is useful in indigestion, etc., being an aerated solution of carbonate of magnesia. It is an agreeable mode of taking magnesia.

Potass Water

Is a solution of bicarbonate of potass in distilled water, and aerated with washed carbonic acid gas.

Soda Water

Is a solution of crystallized carbonate of soda, in distilled water, aerated with washed carbonic acid gas, upon the purity of which the excellence of this article mainly depends. When employed as an anti-acid, it is highly important to obtain this article pure.

Seltzer Water

Is carbonate of soda, common salt, and carbonate of magnesia.

Effervescent Draught.

Carbonate of potass, eighty grains; pulverized citric acid, seventeen grains. Keep separate. When required for use, add one drop of essence of lemon. Dissolve in separate tumblers, mix and drink while effervescing.

Soda-Water Powders.

Bicarbonate of soda, thirty grains, in a blue paper; citric acid twenty-four grains, in a white paper. Mix each separately in nearly half a tumbler of water. Pour the acid solution on the soda. Drink immediately.

FRUIT WINES.

Cherry Wine.

35 lbs. ripe cherries.
5 lbs. brown sugar.
Water, sufficient to make 8 gallons.
1¼ pints best French brandy.
Add yeast, and set aside to ferment.

Red Currant Wine.

70 lbs. red currants, bruised and pressed.
10 lbs. brown sugar.
Water, sufficient to fill up a fifteen-gallon cask.
Ferment.

This yields a pleasant red wine, rather tart, but keeps well.

Elderberry Wine.

8 gallons elderberries.
12 gallons water.
60 lbs. brown sugar.

Dissolve, by boiling ; add yeast and ferment ; then add brandy four pounds ; and bung it up for three months. Disagreeable when cold, but if mulled with allspice and drank warm in winter time, it forms a useful stimulant.

Gooseberry Wine.

7 lbs. brown sugar.
40 lb. gooseberries.
Rain water to make ten gallons.
1 quart brandy
Ferment.

Orange Wine.

23 lbs. sugar.
10 gallons water ; boil.
Clarify with the white of six eggs ; pour the boiling liquid upon the parings of one hundred oranges, add the strained juice of these oranges, and yeast, six ounces ; let it work for three or four days, then strain it into a barrel ; bung it up loosely ; in a month add four pounds of brandy, and in three months it will be fit to drink.

Birch Wine.

In February or March, bore holes in birch trees, and when you have secured 9 gallons juice, boil and skim, cooling it down to 100 degrees Fahrenheit. Dissolve in it 9 pounds sugar, adding two ounces lemon, cut fine ; produce fermentation with 1 pint of gluten. Keep keg full constantly, when the fermenting is over, draw it off and strain, or filter into another keg in which you have burned a piece of brimstone paper.

Blackberry Wine.

½ ounce ground cinnamon.
¼ ounce ground cloves.

1 drachm cardamom seeds.
1 drachm grated nutmeg.
5 gallons blackberries.

Mash the berries, pour on 5 gallons water, heat all to a boiling point but do not let it boil.

Add 1½ galls. white syrup; pour all into a 10 gallon keg, keep in a warm place, keep keg full, and after fermenting, strain and press, add one gallon neutral spirits, filter or fine all, and when clear, bottle, and you will have the best.

Black Currant Wine.

5 gallons black currants.
5 gallons water.
10 pounds crushed sugar.

Dissolve sugar in the water. Heat all to 100 degrees Fahrenheit.

Pour into a 10-gallon keg, put in a warm place, keep it constantly full. After fermenting, strain and press; add one gallon spirits, 95 per cent. above proof; fine or filter, and bottle when clear.

Bottling Wines.

Never bottle on a cloudy day; wines never look as transparent as when bottled on a clear day. Never add water to wine that is too strong, unless it has been boiled.

Ginger Wine.

3 gallons water.
3 pounds sugar.
4 ounces Jamaica ginger.
Boil one hour. Strain. Add 3 lemons chopped fine, and half a pint of yeast.

Mix together and pour into a keg. After it has fermented 1 week, draw it; it is ready for use.

Grape Wine.

Pick over carefully, thoroughly ripe grapes, free from stems and blemishes, press out the juice; to one quart of juice add one quart of water, (soft, boiled water is best,) add 1¼ pounds sugar. After it is done fermenting, bung up tight. It will be ready to draw off in 3 months or sooner, but will be a far better wine in a year, if left unmolested until then.

Parsnip Wine.

18 pounds of sweet parsnips.
3 gallons of water.
Boil together soft, press liquor through a sieve, add to each gill 3 pounds loaf sugar; when nearly cold add yeast. Let the wine stand open ten days, stirring from the bottom, several times each day.

Then put it in a cask, and keep it full up to the bung with liquor reserved for that purpose, as it works out.

NEW AND UP-TO-DATE DRINKS.

Liberal Cocktail.

- $\frac{1}{3}$ Pecon bitters.
- $\frac{1}{3}$ whiskey.
- $\frac{1}{3}$ Italian vermouth.
- 3 or 4 dashes of absinthe.

Bamboo Cocktail.

- 1 dash of orange bitters.
- $\frac{2}{3}$ sherry.
- $\frac{1}{3}$ Italian vermouth.

Coronation Cocktail.

- 4 dashes of Peychaud bitters.
- $\frac{2}{3}$ Plymouth gin.
- $\frac{1}{3}$ Italian vermouth.

Milo Cocktail.

- 4 dashes of pepsin bitters.
- $\frac{2}{3}$ Plymouth gin.
- $\frac{1}{3}$ Italian vermouth.

Blackthorn Cocktail.

2 dashes of orange bitters.
⅔ Sloe gin.
⅓ Italian vermouth.

Broadway Cocktail.

4 or 5 dashes of pepsin bitters.
1 drink of French brandy.

Marguerite Cocktail.

1 dash of orange bitters.
⅔ Plymouth gin.
⅓ French vermouth.

Sloe Gin Cocktail.

1 dash Angostura bitters.
1 drink of Sloe gin.

Stewart Cocktail.

½ dash of Angostura bitters.
⅔ Sloe gin.
⅓ Plymouth gin.

Star Cocktail.

1 dash of orange bitters.
⅔ apple jack.
⅓ Italian vermouth.

Rob Roy Cocktail.

1 dash of orange bitters.
⅔ Scotch whiskey.
⅓ Italian vermouth.

Egg Lemonade.

Juice of 1 lemon.
1 egg.
Fill up with plain water, shake well, and serve.

Gin Daisy.

3 dashes of rasberry syrup.
4 dashes of lime juice.
1 drink of dry gin.
3 lumps of ice.
Fruit, and fill up with carbonic.

Whiskey Daisy.

Same as gin, using whiskey.

Gin Rickey.

(Bar glass.)

½ lime.
1 lump of ice.
1 drink of dry gin.
Fill with carbonic.

Sloe Gin Rickey.

Same as gin rickey, using Sloe gin instead.

Whiskey Rickey.

Same as Sloe gin rickey, using whiskey instead.

Mamie Taylor.

(Large glass.)

Juice of 1 lime.
1 drink of Scotch whiskey.
2 lumps of ice.
1 bottle of imported giner ale.

Mamie Gilroy.

Same as Mamie Taylor; plain soda used instead.

Rimson Cooler.

Peel of 1 lemon.
1 drink of Plymouth gin.
2 lumps of ice.
1 bottle of plain soda.

Horse's Neck.

Peel of 1 lemon.
Bottle of imported ginger ale.
3 or 4 lumps of ice.

Horse's Collar.

Same as Horse's Neck, using a drink of rye whiskey.

Frisco.

1 drink of absinthe and bottle of plain soda.

New and Popular Books sent Free of Postage at Prices Annexed.

CORRECT MANNERS.—A complete hand-book of Etiquette. By
J. B. This book gives much valuable information regard-
ing modern etiquette, rules, usages, manners and customs
of polite society; together with a department under the
head of "Etiquette in a Nut-shell," being fifteen concise
rules; also "George Washington's Life Maxims." It is
one of the best hand-books of the sort ever offered to the
public The illustration gives a fair idea of the shape of
the work.

From Godey's Magazine, November, 1892: "CORRECT
MANNERS.—By J. B. About fifty million Americans need
this book. It is small enough to hide in a coat pocket, yet it contains
about 200 closely printed pages, which begin with twenty-five paragraphs
collectively entitled 'Etiquette in a Nut-shell.' After these come 'George
Washington's Life Maxims,' which, though old, are hard to improve upon.
Following these are chapters on physical deportment, conversation, taste,
memory, modesty, dress, attention, table-talk, dinners and parties—in
short, almost everything at which men and women desire to appear well,
though few know how. All of the author's suggestions are sensible; there
is no mere fashionable nonsense in them."

This work contains 186 pages. Bound in Alligator. Price....**50 cts.**

HOW TO MAKE A DYNAMO.—By Alfred Crofts. A practical
work for Amateurs and Electricians, containing numerous illustrations
and detailed instructions for constructing Dynamos of all sizes to produce
the Electric Light. Large 12mo. Cloth. Price..................**75 cts.**

EXCELSIOR WEBSTER POCKET DICTIONARY.—
Gives the orthography and definition of about 25,000 words, among which
are many words not usually found in a dictionary of this size. It can be
most conveniently referred to and fits the Pocket, being especially prepared for that purpose. The dictionary is not a reprint, but has been carefully prepared by competent hands to meet the general want for a book
of this kind, and for the space it occupies has no superior in the publishing
world. Containing 320 pages, double column. Size 5 x 3½ inches. Bound
in extra cloth. Price, 25 cts. Indexed..........................**35 cts.**

THE PRACTICAL ANGLER.—How, Where and When to Catch
Fish. By Kit Clarke, Author of "Where the Trout Hide," etc. Giving a
description of all American Game Fish caught with hook and line; methods
of capture; their habits and haunts, and all requisite information whereby
the novice can acquire the art, and enjoy the delightful recreation of going
a fishing. Illustrated. Paper cover, 50 cts. Cloth................**$1.00**

EXCELSIOR PUBLISHING HOUSE,

POPULAR ELECTRICAL BOOKS.

A. B. C. OF ELECTRICITY. By W. H. MEADOWCROFT,
ENDORSED BY THOS. A. EDISON.

This is an excellent primary book. Over 70,000 copies have been sold. The A. B. C. principles upon which electrical science is built are set forth in a clear and concise manner. The information it contains is valuable and correct. It is for every person desiring a knowledge of electricity and is what its title implies the first flight of steps in electricity. *12mo, cloth, illust. Price*, 50c.

A. B. C. OF THE X-RAYS. By W. H. MEADOWCROFT.

This is the best primary work on the subject. The aim of the book is to explain the whole apparatus and the manner of its workings in a popular and practical way.
12mo, cloth, illustrated. Price 75c.

A. B. C. OF ELECTRICAL EXPERIMENTS, By W. J. CLARKE

A practical elementary book adapted to beginners and students; giving plain instructions for the making of batteries, magnets, telegraph, telephone, electric bells, induction coils, X-rays, wireless telegraphy, dynamos and motors. Any student either young or old can procure the material mentioned at small cost, and can make for himself any of the instruments, or can work out the experiments given in this book, thus getting a thorough practical knowledge of the principles which underlie the great science of Electricity. *12mo, cloth, illustrated. Price*, $1 00.

ELECTRICAL INSTRUMENT MAKING FOR AMATEURS.
By S. R. BOTTONE.

Contains plain instructions by which any one moderately handy with tools can make the instruments now employed in theoretical or practical electricity from Torsion balance and induction coils to dynamos, motors, telephone, phonograph and micrograph. *12mo, cloth, illustrated. Price*, 50c.

ELECTRIC BELLS AND ALL ABOUT THEM. By S. R. BOTTONE

In this volume the whole subject of electric bells is explained in simple language. A great help to the professional. An amateur can master it within a very short time.
12mo, cloth, illustrated. Price, 50c.

ELECTRO MOTORS, HOW MADE AND HOW USED.
By S. R. BOTTONE AND A. M. A. BEALE.

A handbook for amateurs and practical men, giving a complete and simple explanation of the source of the power in a motor and the method of applying the same.
12mo, cloth, illustrated. Price, 75c.

HOW TO MAKE A DYNAMO. By ALFRED CROFTS.

A practical work for amateurs and electricians, giving detailed instructions for constructing dynamos and all the parts.
12mo, cloth, illustrated. Price, 75c.

Any of the above books sent postpaid upon receipt of price.

EXCELSIOR PUBLISHING HOUSE,
McKEON & SCHOFIELD, Proprietors. 8 MURRAY ST., NEW YORK

PRACTICAL SELF HELPS.

COURT REPORTING.
A MANUAL OF LEGAL DICTATION AND FORMS.

This book is designed for stenographers and typewriters who are desirous of becoming proficient and expert in law work and court reporting. It contains all the various forms of legal matter that are dictated to a stenographer in a law office or court, and are taken from actual business dictated by our most prominent lawyers and judges, which makes the book a valuable work, both for self and class instruction. The highest state of proficiency can be attained in stenography and typewriting through the practice offered by this book. The book also contains a list of legal words and phrases, with their abbreviations, which are in constant use in law work, together with a full and complete spelling list of 28,000 words. 12mo. Bound in Half Law Sheep. Price.........$1.00.

BROWN'S BUSINESS CORRESPONDENCE AND MANUAL OF DICTATION.

For the use of teachers and students of stenography and typewriting. Containing selected letters of actual correspondence in banking, insurance, railroad, and mercantile business; a chapter on punctuation, spelling, and use of capital letters; together with a full and complete spelling list of 25,000 words. 12mo. Cloth. Price, $1.00.

LAW AT A GLANCE; OR, EVERY MAN HIS OWN COUNSELOR.

A new epitome of the laws of the different States of our Union and those of the General Government of the United States, and will be found invaluable to those who are forced to appeal to the law, as well as the large class who wish to avoid it. The whole is alphabetically arranged so as to make reference to it easy. 12mo. Half Law Sheep. Price...................................$1.00.

BOOKKEEPING AT A GLANCE.
By Expert J. T. BRIERLY.

A simple and concise method of practical bookkeeping, with instructions for the proper keeping of books of accounts, and numerous explanations and forms used in commercial business, showing an entire set of books based upon actual transactions, how to take off a trial balance sheet, and finally close and balance accounts. Also Catechism of Bookkeeping—being conversation between teacher and student. Containing 144 pages. Small 16mo. Russian leather. Price, 50 cents. Russian leather, gilt, indexed. Price, 75 cents.

Any of the above books sent postpaid upon receipt of price.

EXCELSIOR PUBLISHING HOUSE,
McKEON & SCHOFIELD, Proprietors. 8 MURRAY ST., NEW YORK.

GERMAN AT A GLANCE.
"Sprechen Sie Deutsch?"

A new system, on the most simple principles, for Universal Self-Tuition, with English pronunciation of every word. By this system any person can become proficient in the German language in a very short time. It is the most complete and easy method ever published. By FRANZ THIMM. (Revised Edition.)

Bound in paper cover. Price................ 25 cts.

FRENCH AT A GLANCE.
"Parlez vous Francais?"

Uniform and arranged the same as "German at a Glance," being the most thorough and easy system for Self-Tuition. (Revised Edition.)

Bound in paper cover. Price................ 25 cts.

SPANISH AT A GLANCE.
"¿Habla V. Espanol?"

A new system for Self-Tuition, arranged the same as French and German, being the easiest method of acquiring a thorough knowledge of the Spanish language. (Revised Edition.)

Bound in paper cover. Price................ 25 cts.

ITALIAN AT A GLANCE.
"Parlate Italiano?"

Uniform in size and style with German, French, and Spanish, being the most simple method of learning the Italian language. (Revised Edition.)

Price................ 25 cts.

Classic Cocktail Resource Guide

Some ingredients found in vintage cocktail guides are unavailable or hard to come by today. However, the creation of historically accurate cocktails is a growing hobby and with a bit of Internet research, you will find recipes for bitters and syrups online, as well as manufacturers that are developing new product lines for the classic cocktail enthusiast.

Vendors
A short selection of online vendors selling herbs, bitters, mixers, syrups, wine, liqueurs, and spirits. This list is by no means complete but is a good place to start your search.

BevMo!
www.bevmo.com

Binny's Beverage Depot
www.binnys.com

The Bitter Truth
www.the-bitter-truth.com

Cocktail Kingdom
www.cocktailkingdom.com

Fee Brothers
www.feebrothers.com

Hi-Time Wine Cellars
www.hitimewine.net

Internet Wines and Spirits
www.internetwines.com

The Jug Shop
www.thejugshop.com

Monin Gourmet Flavorings
www.moninstore.com

Mountain Rose Herbs
www.mountainroseherbs.com

Trader Tiki's Hand-Crafted Exotic Syrups
www.tradertiki.com

The Whiskey Exchange
www.thewhiskyexchange.com

General Interest

These sites provide background information on individual ingredients, suggestions for substitutes, current commercial availability, and recipes.

The Chanticleer Society
A Worldwide Organization of Cocktail Enthusiasts
www.chanticleersociety.org

Drink Boy
Adventures in Cocktails
www.drinkboy.com

The Internet Cocktail Database Ingredients Search
www.cocktaildb.com/ingr_search

Museum of the American Cocktail
www.museumoftheamericancocktail.org

WebTender Wiki
www.wiki.webtender.com

Coming Soon from
Classic Cocktail Guides
and Retro Bartender Books

Home Made Beverages

The Manufacture of Non-Alcoholic and Alcoholic Drinks in the Household, Including Recipes for Essences, Extracts, and Syrups

A Pre-Prohibition Cocktail Book

Albert Hopkins

Classic Cocktail Guides
and Retro Bartender Books

Cooling Cups
and Dainty Drinks

A Collection of 19th-Century Cocktails Perfect
for Civil War Reenactments
and Victorian Theme Parties

William Terrington

Illustrations from
"American Dancing Master and Ball-Room Prompter"
by Elias Howe

ISBN: 978-1-880954-35-5

Classic Cocktail Guides
and Retro Bartender Books

Jack's Manual of Recipes for Fancy Mixed Drinks and How to Serve Them

A Pre-Prohibition Cocktail Book

J. A. Grohusko

ISBN: 978-1-880954-28-7

Classic Cocktail Guides
and Retro Bartender Books

Daly's Bartender's Encyclopedia

A Pre-Prohibition Cocktail Book

Tim Daly

ISBN: 978-1-880954-32-4

Historic Cookbooks of the World

Recipes of the Highlands and Islands of Scotland

A Classic Scottish Cookbook

Compiled by
An Comunn Gaidhealach

Originally published as
"The Feill Cookery Book"

ISBN: 978-1-880954-25-6

Historic Cookbooks of the World

Recipes of Sweden

A Classic Swedish Cookbook

Compiled by
Inga Norberg

Originally published as
"Good Food from Sweden"

ISBN: 978-1-880954-27-0

www.ingramcontent.com/pod-product-compliance
Lightning Source LLC
Chambersburg PA
CBHW031446040426
42444CB00007B/996